THREE PLAYS

Plays by Eugène Ionesco

THE LESSON
THE CHAIRS
THE BALD PRIMA DONNA
JACQUES *Or* OBEDIENCE
AMEDEE *Or* HOW TO GET RID OF IT
THE NEW TENANT
VICTIMS OF DUTY
THE KILLER
IMPROVISATION
MAID TO MARRY
RHINOCEROS
THE LEADER
THE FUTURE IS IN EGGS
Or IT TAKES ALL SORTS TO MAKE A WORLD
THE STROLLER IN THE AIR
THE KING DIES
THE MOTOR SHOW
QUARTET
TWO'S DELIGHT

PLAYS

EUGÈNE IONESCO

THE CHAIRS
THE KILLER
MAID TO MARRY

translated by
DONALD WATSON

A Jupiter Book

LONDON

JOHN CALDER

THESE PLAYS FIRST PUBLISHED IN GREAT BRITAIN IN 1958 & REPRINTED IN 1960
BY JOHN CALDER (PUBLISHERS) LIMITED
17 SACKVILLE STREET, LONDON, W.I

PUBLISHED AS A JUPITER BOOK IN 1963

PRINTED IN GREAT BRITAIN BY
LATIMER, TREND AND CO. LTD., PLYMOUTH

THE CHAIRS

THE CHAIRS

A TRAGIC FARCE

First produced in Paris by Sylvain Dhomme at the Théâtre Lancry, the 22nd April, 1952.

First performed in London by the English Stage Company at the Royal Court Theatre, the 14th May, 1957. Producer, Tony Richardson.

CHARACTERS

> THE OLD MAN, ninety-five years old.
> THE OLD WOMAN, ninety-four years old.
> THE ORATOR, forty-five to fifty years old.
> And many other characters.

SET

> *Circular walls, with a recess at the rear of the stage. The stage is very bare. On the right, starting from the front of the stage, there are three doors. Then a window, with a stool in front of it; then another door. In the recess at the rear, a great monumental double door and two other ordinary ones, facing each other, on both sides of it: these two doors, or one of them at least, are hidden from the public. On the left of the stage, still starting from the front, there are three doors, a window with a stool right opposite the right-hand window, then a blackboard and a platform. The accompanying sketch makes the plan clearer. Centre, down-stage, there are two chairs, side by side. A gas-lamp is suspended from the ceiling.*
>
> *The curtain rises. Semi-darkness. The OLD MAN is standing on the stool leaning out of the left-hand window. The OLD WOMAN is lighting the gas-lamp. A green light. She goes and pulls the OLD MAN's sleeve.*

7

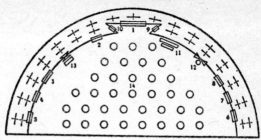

OLD WOMAN: Hurry up, dear, and close the window. I don't like the smell of stagnant water, and the mosquitoes are coming in, too.

OLD MAN: Don't fuss!

OLD WOMAN: Come along now, dear, come and sit down. Don't lean out like that, you might fall in. You know what happened to Francis I. You must be careful.

OLD MAN: Another of your historical allusions! I'm tired of French history, my love. I want to look. The boats in the sunshine are like specks on the water.

OLD WOMAN: You can't see them, it's night-time, my pet, there is no sun.

OLD MAN: It's still casting shadows, anyway. [*He leans right out.*]

OLD WOMAN: [*pulling him back with all her might*] Ah! . . . You're frightening me, my dear . . . come and sit down, you won't see them coming. It's no use trying. It's dark. . . . [*The* OLD MAN *reluctantly lets her pull him away.*]

OLD MAN: I wanted to look. I *do* so enjoy looking at the water.

OLD WOMAN: How can you, dear? . . . It makes *me* quite giddy. Oh! This house, this island, I shall never get used to it all. Water all round you . . . water under the windows, water as far as the eye can see. [*The* OLD WOMAN

8

pulls the OLD MAN *forward to the two chairs at the front of the stage; the* OLD MAN *sits down on the* OLD WOMAN'S *lap, as though it were the most natural thing in the world.*]

OLD MAN: Six o'clock in the evening and it's dark already. Remember? It was different in the old days; it was still light at nine o'clock, at ten o'clock, at midnight.

OLD WOMAN: So it was! What a memory you've got!

OLD MAN: It's all changed now.

OLD WOMAN: Do you know why it's changed?

OLD MAN: No, I don't, Semiramis, my pet. . . . Perhaps, because the further we go, the deeper the rut. It's all on account of the earth, which never stops turning, turning, turning. . . .

OLD WOMAN: Turning, turning, my love. . . . [*Silence.*] Oh yes! You really are a great scholar. You're so clever, my dear. You might have become a President General, a General Director, or even a General Physician or a Postmaster-General, if you'd wanted to, if you'd had just a little ambition in life. . . .

OLD MAN: What good would that have done us? We shouldn't have had a better life . . . after all, we have a job to do, since I'm a caretaker, I am a Quartermaster-General.

OLD WOMAN: [*she fondles the* OLD MAN *as if he were a child*] My little pet, angel child. . . .

OLD MAN: I'm so tired of everything.

OLD WOMAN: You were more cheerful when you were looking at the water. . . . Just to cheer us up, let's pretend, as we did the other night.

OLD MAN: Pretend yourself, it's your turn.

OLD WOMAN: It isn't, it's yours.

OLD MAN: It isn't.

OLD WOMAN: It is.

OLD MAN: It isn't.

OLD WOMAN: It is.

OLD MAN: Semiramis, drink your tea. [*Naturally, there is no tea.*]

OLD WOMAN: Imitate February, then.

OLD MAN: I don't like the months of the year.

OLD WOMAN: There's no other kind at the moment. Go on, just to please me. . . .

OLD MAN: All right, then. This is February. [*He scratches his head, like Stan Laurel.*]

OLD WOMAN: [*clapping and laughing*] Yes, that's it! Oh thank you, thank you, you really are a sweet little pet. [*She kisses him.*] You're *so* clever, you could have been at least a Postmaster-General, if you'd wanted to. . . .

OLD MAN: I'm a caretaker, a Quartermaster-General. [*Silence.*]

OLD WOMAN: Tell me the story. You know, *the* story: and then we arri . . .

OLD MAN: What again? . . . I'm tired of it . . . and then we arri? That one again? You always ask me for the same thing! . . . 'And then we arri . . .'. It's so boring. . . . Every evening, every evening without exception, through seventy-five years of married life, you make me tell the same story, imitate the same people, the same months . . . always the same . . . let's change the subject. . . .

OLD WOMAN: I never get tired of it, my love. . . . It's *your* life, so exciting.

OLD MAN: You know it by heart.

OLD WOMAN: It's as if I forget everything straightaway. . . . Every evening I start with a fresh mind. . . . But I do, my pet, I do it on purpose. I take a purge. . . . I'm as good as new again, just for you, my dear, every evening. . . . Please hurry up and begin.

OLD MAN: All right, then.

OLD WOMAN: Come on, start telling your story. . . . Of course it's mine as well: what's yours is mine! Then we arri . . .

OLD MAN: Then we arri . . . my pet . . .

OLD WOMAN: Then we arri . . . my love . . .

OLD MAN: Then we arrived at a great iron gate. We'd been soaked to the skin, frozen to the bone, for hours, for days, for nights, for weeks . . .

OLD WOMAN: For months . . .

OLD MAN: . . . In the rain. . . . We were chattering all over, our ears, our feet, our knees, our noses, our teeth . . . that was eighty years ago now. . . . They wouldn't let us in . . . They might at least have opened the garden gate. [*Silence.*]

OLD WOMAN: In the garden the grass was wet.

OLD MAN: There was a path that led to a little square. And in the middle a village church. . . . Where was that village? Do you remember?

OLD WOMAN: No, my dear, I've forgotten.

OLD MAN: How did we get there? Where's the road to it? I believe the place was called Paris . . .

OLD WOMAN: Paris? There never was such a place, my pet.

OLD MAN: There must have been once, because it fell into ruins. . . . It was the city of light and four hundred thousand years ago it faded right away . . . there's nothing left of it now, except a song.

OLD WOMAN: A real song? That's funny. What is it?

OLD MAN: A lullaby, a parable: 'Paris will always be Paris.'

OLD WOMAN: Did we get there through the garden? Was it a long way?

OLD MAN: [*dreamily, far away*] The song? . . . the rain? . . .

OLD WOMAN: You're so clever. If you'd had just a little ambition in life, you might have become a General Editor, an Attorney-General, a General Postmaster-General . . . Oh dear, all swept away under the bridge . . . under the great black bridge of time . . . swept away, I tell you. [*Silence.*]

OLD MAN: And then we arri . . .

OLD WOMAN: Oh yes! Go on with the story . . .

OLD MAN: [*while the* OLD WOMAN *begins to laugh quietly, crazily, gradually working up into fits of laughter. The* OLD MAN *laughs, too.*] And then we arrived and we laughed till we cried to see the funny man arrive with his hat all awry . . . it was so funny when he fell flat on his face, he had such a fat tummy . . . he arrived with a case full of rice: the rice on the ground, all awry . . . we laughed till we cried . . . and we cried and cried . . . funny fat tummy, rice on a wry face, flat on his rice, case full of face . . . and we laughed till we cried . . . funny hat flat on his fat face, all awry . . .

OLD WOMAN: [*laughing*] . . . arrived on his rice, face all awry, and we cried when we arrived, case, face, tummy, fat, rice . . .

BOTH: [*together, laughing*] And then we arri. Ah! . . . arri . . . arri . . . Ah! . . . Ah! . . . ri . . . ri . . . rice . . . awry . . . fat hat awry . . . fat tummy funny . . . rice arrived awry . . . [*And then we hear:*] And then we . . . fat tummy . . . arri . . . the case . . . [*And the* OLD COUPLE *slowly quieten down.*] Cried . . . ah! . . . arrived . . . ah! . . . arri . . . a . . . wry . . . rice . . . face.

OLD WOMAN: So that was your famous old Paris.

OLD MAN: Parasite lost.

OLD WOMAN: Oh! you *are*, my dear, oh you *are* really, you are *so* . . . so . . . you could have been something in life, much more than a Quartermaster-General.

OLD MAN: Don't let us be boastful . . . we should be satisfied with the little we have . . .

OLD WOMAN: Perhaps you've wrecked your career?

OLD MAN: [*suddenly starts crying*] Wrecked it? Dashed it to pieces? Broken it? Oh! Where are you, mummy? Mummy, where are you? . . . hee, hee, hee, I'm an orphan. [*Groaning.*] . . . an orphan, a norphan . . .

OLD WOMAN: Mummy's with you, what are you afraid of?

OLD MAN: No, Semiramis, my pet. You're not my mummy . . . an orphan, a norphan, who will look after me?

OLD WOMAN: But I'm still here, my love! . . .

OLD MAN: That's not the same . . . I want my mummy, so there! You're not my mummy.

OLD WOMAN: [*stroking him*] You're breaking my heart. Don't cry, little one.

OLD MAN: Hee, hee! Leave me alone; hee, hee! I feel all cracked and smashed, I've a pain, my career is hurting me, it's all in pieces.

OLD WOMAN: There, there!

OLD MAN: [*sobbing, with his mouth wide open, like a baby*] I'm an orphan . . . a norphan.

OLD WOMAN: [*trying to coax him into being quiet*] My little orphan boy, you're breaking mummy's heart, my pet. [*She has already started rocking the disillusioned old man backwards and forwards on her knees.*]

OLD MAN [*sobbing*] Hee, hee, hee! Mummy! Where's my mummy? I've lost my mummy.

OLD WOMAN: I'm your wife, so now I'm your mummy, too.

OLD MAN: [*giving in a little*] It's not true, I'm an orphan, hee, hee.

OLD WOMAN: [*still rocking him*] My little sweetheart, my little orphan, norphan, porphan, borphan, morphan.

OLD MAN: [*still sulky, but coming round slowly*] No . . . I don't want to, I wo-o-on't!

OLD WOMAN: [*singing softly*] Anorphan-lee, anorphan-lo, anorphan-lah, anorphan-lu, anorphan-lay.

OLD MAN: No-o-o-o . . . No-o-o-o.

OLD WOMAN: [*as before*] Leelo, lahlo, lulo, lay, norphan-lo, morphan-lu, borphan-lee, porphan-lay . . .

OLD MAN: Hee, hee, hee, hee. [*He sniffs and gradually calms down.*] Where is she, my mummy ?

OLD WOMAN: In the gardens of Paradise . . . she can hear you, and see you, peeping out from among the flowers; you mustn't cry or you'll make her cry too!

OLD MAN: It's not *true* . . . she *can't* see me, she *can't* hear me. I'm an orphan, for life, and you're not my real mummy . . .

OLD WOMAN: [*the* OLD MAN *is almost calm now*] There now, you see you've nothing to worry about. . . . My little General's a very clever boy . . . dry those tears away, all the guests will be here this evening and we mustn't let them see you like this . . . you haven't smashed everything, there's still some hope left; you'll tell them all about it, you can explain it all: *You've* got a *message* . . . you're always saying you're going to pass it on . . . you must live and fight for your message . . .

OLD MAN: I've a message, you're right, I must fight for it, a mission, I can give birth to a great idea, a message for all men, for all mankind . . .

OLD WOMAN: For all mankind, my dear, your message! . . .

OLD MAN: It's true, that's really true . . .

OLD WOMAN: [*blowing the* OLD MAN's *nose and wiping away his tears*] That's the way! . . . You're a big boy now, a real soldier, a Quartermaster-General . . .

OLD MAN: [*he has got off the* OLD WOMAN's *knees and is trotting*

14

about excitedly] I'm not like other people. I've an ideal in life. I may be clever, as you say. I am quite talented, but things don't come easily to me. I've carried out my duties as Quartermaster-General satisfactorily, proved myself equal to the task, come out of it quite honourably, that ought to be enough . . .

OLD WOMAN: Not for you, you're not like other men, you're greater than they are; and yet you'd have done much better if you'd got on well with everyone else, like everyone else. You quarrelled with all your friends, with all the directors, all the Generals, and with your own brother.

OLD MAN: Wasn't my fault, Semiramis, you know what he said.

OLD WOMAN: What did he say?

OLD MAN: He said: My dear friends, I've caught a flea somewhere, and I've come to see *you* in the hope of losing it again.

OLD WOMAN: Everyone says that, my love. You shouldn't have taken any notice. But why did you get upset with Karl? Was that his fault, too?

OLD MAN: You'll make me lose my temper, lose my temper. So there! Of course it was his fault. He came along one evening and this is what he said: 'Best of luck, old Kangaroo. I wish you every success and hope you get what's coming to you.' And he bellowed like a horse.

OLD WOMAN: He meant well, dear. It doesn't do to be so sensitive in life.

OLD MAN: I don't like that sort of joke.

OLD WOMAN: You could have been a General Decorator, a General in the Navy, or a General Factotum. [*A long silence. For a while they are quite motionless, sitting rigidly in their chairs.*]

OLD MAN: [*dreamily*] It was at the bottom of the bottom of

the garden . . . and *there* was a . . . *there* was a . . . *there* was a . . . *what* was there, my pet?

OLD WOMAN: The city of Paris, of course!

OLD MAN: At the end, at the end of the end of the city of Paris, was, was, was what?

OLD WOMAN: Old friend, was what, old friend, was who?

OLD MAN: The place and the weather were perfect, too.

OLD WOMAN: Was the weather really so hot?

OLD MAN: What the place was like I quite forgot . . .

OLD WOMAN: Forget it, then, if it worries you . . .

OLD MAN: It's too far away, I can't, I can't . . . bring it back . . . where was it?

OLD WOMAN: Was what?

OLD MAN: What I . . . What you . . . where was it? and who?

OLD WOMAN: Wherever it was, whatever it was, I'd come with you, old friend, to the end, I'd follow you.

OLD MAN: Ah! I find it so difficult to express myself . . . and I *must* tell everything, too.

OLD WOMAN: It's your sacred duty. You haven't the right to keep your message to yourself; you must reveal it to mankind, everyone's waiting for it . . . the whole universe is waiting just for you.

OLD MAN: Yes, yes, I'll do it.

OLD WOMAN: You've really decided? You must.

OLD MAN: Drink your tea.

OLD WOMAN: You might have been an Orator-General, if you'd had a little more will-power in life . . . I am proud and happy to hear that at last you've decided to speak to all the countries of Europe, to all the continents in the world!

OLD MAN: But I find it so difficult to express myself; things don't come easily to me.

OLD WOMAN: Once you begin, things come easily enough, like life and death . . . you just have to make up your mind. It's as we speak that we find our ideas, our words, ourselves, too, in our own words, and the city, the garden, perhaps everything comes back and we're not orphans any more.

OLD MAN: I shan't do the talking myself, I've engaged a professional orator to speak in my name, you'll see.

OLD WOMAN: So it's really going to be this evening? I suppose you've invited everybody? All the important people, all the property-owners and all the scientists?

OLD MAN: Yes, all the learned and the landed. [*Silence.*]

OLD WOMAN: The wardens? the bishops? the chemists? the boiler-makers? the violinists? the shop-stewards? the presidents? the constables? the tradesmen? the public buildings? the penholders? the chromosomes?

OLD MAN: Yes, yes, and the postmen, the typists and the artists, anyone who could be called a scientist or a property-owner.

OLD WOMAN: And the bankers?

OLD MAN: I've invited *them*.

OLD WOMEN: The proletarians? the parliamentarians? the functionaries? the reactionaries? the revolutionaries? the mental specialists and the mental patients?

OLD MAN: All of them, of course, all of them; they're all scientists and property-owners.

OLD WOMAN: Don't get so angry, my love. I didn't mean to upset you, but like all men of genius you are so forgetful; this meeting's important, they must come this evening, all of them. Are you sure they will? Did they promise?

OLD MAN: Drink your tea, Semiramis. [*Silence.*]

OLD WOMAN: The Pope, the popinjays, and the papers?

OLD MAN: I've invited them too. [*Silence.*] I shall deliver

17

them my message . . . All my life I felt I was suffocating; and now they'll know everything, thanks to you and the Orator, the only people who have understood me.

OLD WOMAN: I'm so proud of you . . .

OLD MAN: The meeting will soon be starting.

OLD WOMAN: So it's really true, they're going to come this evening? You won't want to cry any more. When we've got scientists and property-owners, we don't need daddies and mummies. [*Silence.*] We couldn't put the meeting off now. I hope it doesn't make us too tired! [*The excitement is mounting. The* OLD MAN *has already started trotting round the* OLD WOMAN, *with short, uncertain steps, like a child's or a very old man's. He has already succeeded in taking a few steps towards one of the doors, but has come back to go round her again.*]

OLD MAN: You really think we shall find it tiring?

OLD WOMAN: You *have* got a bit of a cold.

OLD MAN: How could we postpone it?

OLD WOMAN: Let's invite them for another evening. You could telephone them.

OLD MAN: Don't be silly. I can't, it's too late. They must be on the boats by now!

OLD WOMAN: You oughtn't to have been so rash. [*A boat can be heard slipping through the water.*]

OLD MAN: I believe that's someone already . . . [*The noise gets louder.*] . . . Yes, someone's coming! . . . [*The* OLD WOMAN *gets up too and hobbles about.*]

OLD WOMAN: Perhaps it's the Orator.

OLD MAN: He wouldn't be in such a hurry. It must be someone else. [*A bell rings.*] Ah!

OLD WOMAN: Ah! [*Nervously the* OLD COUPLE *make for the concealed door backstage right. As they move, they go on talking:*]

OLD MAN: Come along . . .

OLD WOMAN: I haven't combed my hair . . . wait a moment

. . . [*She tidies her hair and straightens her dress as she hobbles along, pulling up her thick red stockings.*]

OLD MAN: You ought to have got ready before . . . you had plenty of time.

OLD WOMAN: What a sight I look . . . such an old frock on, all creased up . . .

OLD MAN: You'd only got to iron it . . . hurry up! You're keeping people waiting. [*The* OLD MAN *reaches the door in the recess, followed by the grumbling* OLD WOMAN; *for a moment they disappear from sight; they can be heard opening the door and then shutting it again, as they let someone in.*]

OLD WOMAN'S VOICE: Good evening, Madam, very pleased to make your acquaintance. Be careful, don't spoil your hat. You can take out the hat-pin, you'll feel more comfortable. Oh no! No one will sit on it.

OLD MAN'S VOICE: Put your fur down there. Let me help you. No, it will come to no harm.

OLD WOMAN'S VOICE: Oh! What a pretty suit . . . a blouse in red, white and blue. . . . You will have some biscuits, won't you? . . . But you're not fat . . . no . . . just plump . . . Do put your umbrella down.

OLD MAN'S VOICE: Will you come this way, please?

OLD MAN: [*his back to the audience*] My job is a very ordinary one . . . [*The* OLD COUPLE *turn to face the audience at the same time, moving a little apart to leave room for the* LADY GUEST *between them. She is invisible. The* OLD COUPLE *now come forward to the front of the stage, as they talk to the invisible* LADY *between them.*]

OLD MAN: [*to the invisible* LADY] Have you been having good weather?

OLD WOMAN: [*to the invisible* LADY] You're not feeling too tired? . . . A little, perhaps.

OLD MAN: [*to the invisible* LADY] At the seaside . . .

OLD WOMAN: [*to the invisible* LADY] Really most kind of you.

OLD MAN: [*to the invisible* LADY] I'll bring you a chair. [*The* OLD MAN *goes off left, through Door No. 6.*]

OLD WOMAN: [*to the invisible* LADY] Meanwhile, why don't you sit here? Rather warm, isn't it? [*She points to one of the two chairs and sits down on the other one, on the right side of the invisible* LADY.] What a pretty fan! My husband . . . [*The* OLD MAN *re-appears through Door No. 7, carrying a chair.*] . . . gave me one something like it, seventy-three years ago . . . I still have it . . . [*The* OLD MAN *sets the chair down to the left of the invisible* LADY.] . . . it was a birthday present! . . . [*The* OLD MAN *sits down on the chair he has just brought, so that the invisible* LADY *is in the middle. The* OLD MAN *looks at the* LADY, *smiles at her, nods his head, rubs his hands gently together and appears to be following what she is saying. The* OLD WOMAN *does the same.*]

OLD MAN: Madam, the cost of living has always been high.

OLD WOMAN: [*to the* LADY] You're quite right . . . [*The* LADY *speaks.*] I agree with you. It's time there was a change . . . [*In a different tone of voice.*] My husband may be having something to do with it . . . *he* will tell you.

OLD MAN: [*to the* OLD WOMAN] Ssh! Be quiet, Semiramis, it's not time to talk about it yet. [*To the* LADY:] Forgive me, Madam, for rousing your curiosity. [*The* LADY *reacts to this.*] Dear Lady, please don't insist . . . [*The* OLD COUPLE *smile. They even laugh. They look as if they are enjoying the story the* LADY *is telling. A pause: a lull in the conversation. Their faces have lost all expression.*]

OLD MAN: [*to the* LADY] Oh yes, you're perfectly right . . .

OLD WOMAN: Yes, yes, yes . . . Oh, but no!

OLD MAN: Yes, yes, yes. By all means.

OLD WOMAN: Yes?

OLD MAN: No!?

OLD WOMAN: That's it exactly.

OLD MAN: [*laughing*] It can't be true!

OLD WOMAN: [*to invisible* LADY] Oh well then! [*To the* OLD MAN:] She's delightful.

OLD MAN: [*to* OLD WOMAN] The lady's made a conquest, has she! [*To the* LADY:] Well done!

OLD WOMAN: [*to the* LADY] You're not like the young people of today . . .

OLD MAN: [*he is painfully bending down to pick up an invisible object that the invisible* LADY *has dropped*] No, please . . . please don't trouble yourself . . . I'll pick it up . . . There now! You're quicker than I am . . . [*He straightens up.*]

OLD WOMAN: [*to the* OLD MAN] She's younger than you are!

OLD MAN: [*to the* LADY] Old age is a terrible burden. I wish I could grant you Eternal Youth.

OLD WOMAN: [*to the* LADY] He really means that, it comes straight from his heart. [*To the* OLD MAN:] My pet! [*Silence for a few moments. The* OLD COUPLE *look at the* LADY, *their faces seen in profile, and smile politely; then they look towards the audience, and back again to the* LADY, *smiling in response to her smile; then they answer her questions with the following replies:*]

OLD WOMAN: Most kind of you to take such an interest in us.

OLD MAN: We live a very retired life.

OLD WOMAN: He's not a misanthropist, but my husband likes peace and quiet.

OLD MAN: We have the wireless, I go fishing, and then there's quite a regular ferry service.

OLD WOMAN: There are two boats every Sunday morning and one in the evening, not to speak of the privately-owned ones.

OLD MAN: When the weather's fine, there's a moon.

OLD WOMAN: He still carries out his duties as Quarter-master-General . . . it *does* keep him busy . . . That's true, at his age he could take a little rest.

OLD MAN: I shall have plenty of time for rest when I'm in my grave.

OLD WOMAN: [*to the* OLD MAN] Oh, don't say that, my love! . . . [*To the* LADY:] The family, what's left of it, and my husband's old friends, still used to come and see us from time to time, ten years ago . . .

OLD MAN: [*to the* LADY] In the winter, a good book, sitting by the stove, the memories of a life-time . . .

OLD WOMAN: [*to the* LADY] A simple life, but a full one . . . two hours every day he works at his message. [*A bell rings. The sound of an approaching boat has already been heard.*]

OLD WOMAN: [*to the* OLD MAN] Somebody there. Go quickly.

OLD MAN: [*to the* LADY] Will you excuse me, Madam? I shan't be a moment! [*To the* OLD WOMAN:] Quick! Go and fetch some chairs! [*Someone is pulling the bell furiously.*]

OLD MAN: [*in great haste, very tottery, goes to the door on the right; while the* OLD WOMAN *does her best to hobble quickly to the concealed door on the left.*] Sounds like someone used to giving orders. [*He hurries to open Door No. 2; the invisible* COLONEL *comes in; perhaps it would be a good idea if one could hear, discreetly, a few blasts on a trumpet, a few notes of 'The Colonel's Salute'; as soon as he opens the door, the* OLD MAN *freezes into a respectful position of attention.*] Ah! . . . Colonel! [*He raises his arm vaguely in the direction of his forehead for a salute that is barely recognizable.*] Good evening, Colonel! . . . This is indeed an amazing honour for me . . . I . . . I I never expected . . . although . . . and yet . . . well I'm very proud to see you in my humble abode, such a distinguished hero . . . [*He shakes an invisible hand, held out by the invisible* COLONEL, *bows ceremoniously and then straightens up.*] Nevertheless, without false modesty, may I confess that I do not feel myself entirely unworthy of your visit! Proud, yes . . . but not unworthy . . . ! [*The* OLD WOMAN *appears with a chair, from the right.*]

OLD WOMAN: Oh! What a fine uniform! What pretty decorations! Who is he, my love?

OLD MAN: [*to the* OLD WOMAN] Can't you see it's the Colonel?

OLD WOMAN: [*to the* OLD MAN] Ah!

OLD MAN: [*to the* OLD WOMAN] Count the pips! [*To the* COLONEL:] My wife, Semiramis. [*To the* OLD WOMAN:] Come and be introduced to the Colonel. [*The* OLD WOMAN *comes forward, dragging her chair with her, and makes a curtsey without letting go of it.*] [*To the* COLONEL:] My wife. [*To the* OLD WOMAN:] The Colonel.

OLD WOMAN: So pleased to meet you. A most welcome guest. You are an old friend of my husband's, he's a General . . .

OLD MAN: [*displeased*] Quartermaster, quartermaster . . .

OLD WOMAN: [*the invisible* COLONEL *kisses the* OLD WOMAN'S *hand; this is obvious from the* OLD WOMAN'S *gesture of raising her hand as though to his lips; the* OLD WOMAN *lets the chair fall in her confusion.*] Oh! What a polite man . . . anyone can see he's out of the ordinary, really superior! . . . [*She picks up the chair again; to the* COLONEL:] This chair is for you . . .

OLD MAN: [*to the invisible* COLONEL] I beg you to follow me, Sir . . . [*They all move forward, the* OLD WOMAN *dragging her chair; to the* COLONEL:] Yes, there is someone else here. We're expecting a large number of guests! . . . [*The* OLD WOMAN *places her chair on the right.*]

OLD WOMAN: [*to the* COLONEL] Please take a seat. [*The* OLD MAN *introduces the two invisible characters.*]

OLD MAN: A young lady of our acquaintance . . .

OLD WOMAN: A very good friend of ours . . . renowned in military circles.

OLD MAN: [*as before*] The Colonel . . .

OLD WOMAN: [*indicating the chair she has just brought up for the* COLONEL] Do take this chair . . .

OLD MAN: [*to the* OLD WOMAN] No, no, can't you see the Colonel wants to sit next to the Lady! . . . [*The* COLONEL *sits down invisibly on the third chair from the left; the invisible* LADY *is assumed to be on the second one; an inaudible conversation starts up between the two invisible characters sitting next to each other; the* OLD COUPLE *remain standing behind their chairs, on either side of the two invisible guests: the* OLD MAN *on the left, beside the* LADY, *the* OLD WOMAN *on the right, beside the* COLONEL.]

OLD WOMAN: [*listening to the conversation between the guests*] Oh! Oh! that's going a bit too far.

OLD MAN: Perhaps. [*The* OLD MAN *and the* OLD WOMAN *now make signs to each other, above the heads of the two guests, as they listen to the conversation, which seems to have taken a turn that displeases the* OLD COUPLE. *Suddenly*:] Yes, Sir, they haven't arrived yet, but they're coming. The Orator will be speaking on my behalf, he will explain what my message means . . . Colonel, I really ought to warn you that this lady's husband may be here at any moment.

OLD WOMAN: [*to the* OLD MAN] Who is this gentleman?

OLD MAN: [*to the* OLD WOMAN] I've told you, it's the Colonel. [*Invisibly, something not quite respectable is happening.*]

OLD WOMAN: [*to the* OLD MAN] I knew it.

OLD MAN: Why did you ask me then?

OLD WOMAN: To find out. Your cigarette, Colonel, not on the floor, please!

OLD MAN: Please, Colonel, I've forgotten, Sir. The last war, did you lose it or win it?

OLD WOMAN: [*to the invisible* LADY] But, my dear girl, you can't let him treat you like this!

OLD MAN: [*to the* COLONEL] Take a good look at me, Sir! Don't I look like a real soldier? Once, Colonel, during a battle . . .

OLD WOMAN: That's going much too far! It's not nice! [*Pulling at the* COLONEL's *invisible sleeve.*] Listen to what he's saying now! Do something to stop him, my love!

OLD MAN: [*going quickly on with his story*] All by myself I accounted for 209; that's what we called them, they jumped so high in the air trying to escape, though they weren't quite as thick as flies, not so much fun, of course, Colonel, but thanks to my strength of mind, I killed them . . . Oh no! No, please stop it!

OLD WOMAN: [*to the* COLONEL] My husband never tells a lie: I know we're very old, but we are respectable people.

OLD MAN: [*forcefully to the* COLONEL] If a man wants to be a proper hero, he must have good manners, too!

OLD WOMAN: [*to the* COLONEL] I've known you for a long time now, and I should never have thought it of you. [*To the* LADY, *as more boats are heard:*] I should never have thought it of him. We do have our self-respect, our own personal dignity.

OLD MAN: [*in a very quavery voice*] I'm not yet past the age when I can carry arms. [*Bell rings.*] Excuse me. I must open the door. [*He makes a clumsy movement and the* LADY's *chair is upset.*] I beg your pardon.

OLD WOMAN: [*rushing forward*] You haven't hurt yourself? [*The* OLD COUPLE *help the invisible* LADY *to her feet.*] Now you're all dirty, look at the dust. [*She helps to dust the* LADY *down. Bell rings again.*]

OLD MAN: I'm so sorry. Please forgive me. [*To the* OLD WOMAN:) Go and bring a chair.

OLD WOMAN: [*to the two invisible* GUESTS] Please excuse us a moment. [*As the* OLD MAN *goes to open Door No. 3, the* OLD WOMAN *goes out through Door No. 5 to look for a chair, and will come back through Door No. 8.*]

OLD MAN: [*as he makes for the door*] He wanted to put me in a rage. I almost feel cross with him. [*He opens the door.*] Why, it's you, Madam! I can hardly believe my own eyes, and yet I . . . I really wasn't expecting you . . . really it's . . . Oh, how can you say that. . . . When I've been thinking about you all my life, all my life, Madam, you were known as the Lovely Miss . . . so this is your husband . . . I did hear about it, of course . . . you haven't changed at all . . . yes, perhaps you're right, your nose really has got longer, it's filled out, too . . . I didn't notice it at first, but now I can see . . . terribly long . . . ah! what a pity! But you didn't do it on purpose . . . how did it happen, then? . . . I see, very gradually . . . oh, I'm sorry, Sir, may I call you a dear friend of mine? You see I knew your wife a long time before you did . . . oh yes, just the same person, but with quite a different nose . . . my congratulations, Sir, you seem to be very much in love. [*The* OLD WOMAN *appears through Door No. 8 with a chair.*] Semiramis, *two* people have arrived, so we need another chair . . . [*The* OLD WOMAN *sets her chair down behind the other four, then goes out through Door No. 8 to come back through Door No. 5 a few minutes later, carrying another chair, which he sets down beside the last one. By then the* OLD MAN *should have brought his guests to her side.*] Do please come and be introduced to the other guests . . . now then, Madam . . . oh! lovely,

lovely Miss Lovely, that's what you were called . . . you're nearly bent double now . . . oh! yes, Sir, she's still very lovely, all the same; such pretty eyes, behind those spectacles; her hair is white, of course, but behind the white hairs, there are brown ones and blue ones, I'm sure there are . . . This way, please. . . . What's this, a present, Sir? For my wife? [*To the* OLD WOMAN, *who has just arrived with the chair:*] Semiramis, this is the lovely, you know, the lovely . . . [*to the* COLONEL *and the first invisible* LADY:] This is Miss, I beg your pardon, Mrs Lovely, don't smile . . . and her husband . . . [*to the* OLD WOMAN:] A friend of my childhood days, I've often told you about her . . .

OLD WOMAN: How do you do?

OLD MAN: And her husband. [*to the invisible* COLONEL *and the first* LADY *again:*]
And her husband . . .

OLD WOMAN: [*curtseying*] Most distinguished. A fine figure of a man, I must say. How do you do, how do you do? [*With a wave of the hand in the direction of the first guests:*] Friends of ours, yes . . .

OLD MAN: [*to the* OLD WOMAN] He's brought you a present. [*The* OLD WOMAN *takes the present.*]

OLD WOMAN: Oh dear! Is it a flower? Or a cradle? A pear-tree? Or a pheasant?

OLD MAN: [*to the* OLD WOMAN] No, no. Can't you see it's a picture? It doesn't matter what it's meant to represent.

OLD WOMAN: Oh yes! Very pleasant! Thank you so much . . . [*To the first invisible* LADY:] Would you like to see it, dear?

OLD MAN: [*to the invisible* COLONEL] Would you like to see it?

OLD WOMAN: [*to* MRS LOVELY'S *husband*] Oh, Doctor, Doctor! I often feel sick, feel hot all over, get cold feet and a cold in the head, have pains and chilblains and wind round my heart, Doctor, Doctor! . . .

OLD MAN: [*to the* OLD WOMAN] This gentleman is not a doctor, he's a photographer.

OLD WOMAN: [*to the first* LADY] If you've had a good look at it, you can hang it up. [*To* OLD MAN:] I don't mind, he's a charming man anyway, quite devastating. [*To the* PHOTOGRAPHER:] I'm not trying to flatter you, but . . . [*The* OLD COUPLE *should now be behind the chairs, very close to each other, almost touching, but back to back: they are both talking; the* OLD MAN *to* MRS. LOVELY, *the* OLD WOMAN *to the* PHOTOGRAPHER. *Every now and again they turn their heads to address a remark to one of the first guests.*]

OLD MAN: [*to* MRS LOVELY] I'm quite overwhelmed . . . You really are you, after all . . . I was in love with you a hundred years ago . . . there's been such a great change in you . . . there's been no change in you at all . . . I loved you then, I love you now . . .

OLD WOMAN: [*to the* PHOTOGRAPHER] Oh! Really, Sir! . . .

OLD MAN: [*to the* COLONEL] I quite agree with you there.

OLD WOMAN: [*to the* PHOTOGRAPHER] Oh, really Sir, really! . . . [*To the first* LADY:] Thank you for hanging it up . . . I'm sorry to have disturbed you. [*The lighting is stronger now. It goes on getting stronger and stronger as more of the invisible guests arrive.*]

OLD MAN: [*almost snivelling, to* MRS LOVELY] Where are the snows of yesteryear?

OLD WOMAN: [*to the* PHOTOGRAPHER] Oh, really! Really! . . . Really! Really! . . .

OLD MAN: [*pointing the first* LADY *out to* MRS LOVELY] A young friend of ours . . . a very sweet girl . . .

OLD WOMAN: [*pointing the* COLONEL *out to the* PHOTOGRAPHER] Yes, he's a Colonel in the Civil Service, cavalry . . . an old friend of my husband's . . . a subordinate, my husband's a General . . .

OLD MAN [*to* MRS LOVELY] Your ears weren't always so pointed! . . . do you remember, my lovely?

OLD WOMAN: [*to the* PHOTOGRAPHER, *mincing grotesquely. She should become more coquettish as the scene goes on: showing her thick red stockings, lifting her numerous skirts, revealing a petticoat full of holes, uncovering her ancient breasts; then, throwing her head back, hands on hips, uttering erotic cries, thrusting her pelvis forward, standing with legs apart, she laughs like an old whore. This aspect of the* OLD WOMAN *is quite different from anything we have seen up to now or are to see later; it should suggest something in the* OLD WOMAN'S *character that normally remains hidden and it vanishes abruptly.*] I'm too old for that now . . . you don't think so?

OLD MAN: [*to* MRS LOVELY, *romantically*] When we were young, the moon was a living planet; ah! yes, yes, if we had dared, but we were only children. Would you like to live those long-lost days again . . . can we go back? Can we go back? Oh, no! no! It's too late now. Time has raced past us like a train. It has left its lines in our skin. Do you think plastic surgery can work miracles? [*To the* COLONEL:] I am a soldier, and so are you; soldiers are always young, generals are like gods . . . [*To* MRS LOVELY:] That's how it ought to be . . . But alas! We have lost everything. We could have been so happy, I tell you; perhaps there are flowers coming up through the snow! . . .

OLD WOMAN: [*to the* PHOTOGRAPHER] Flatterer! Naughty boy! Aah! I look young for my age? You're a dashing little dago, a really exciting man.

OLD MAN: [*to* MRS LOVELY] May I play Tristan to your Isolde? Beauty lies in the heart . . . you see, we could have

had our share of bliss, beauty and eternity . . . eternity . . .
Why didn't we dare? We didn't want it enough . . . now
. . . everything is lost to us, lost, lost, lost.

OLD WOMAN: [*to the* PHOTOGRAPHER] Oh no! Oh! No, oh!
La, la! I'm trembling all over. Are you tickled, too?
Ticklish or just a tickler? I really shouldn't . . . [*She laughs.*]
Do you like my petticoat? Or do you prefer the skirt?

OLD MAN: [*to* MRS LOVELY] It's a wretched life, a Quartermaster-General's!

OLD WOMAN: [*looking towards the first invisible* LADY] How
do you make crêpes de Chine? The egg of an ox, an hour
of flour and some gastric juices. [*To the* PHOTOGRAPHER:]
You've got very feeling fingers, ah! . . . well, I mean to
s-a-a-y! . . . oh-oh-oh-oh!

OLD MAN: [*to* MRS LOVELY] My worthy spouse, Semiramis,
has taken the place of my mother. [*He turns to the* COLONEL.]
But, Colonel, I told you that before: Truth is where you
find it. [*He turns back to* MRS LOVELY.]

OLD WOMAN: [*to the* PHOTOGRAPHER] You really, really
believe you can have children at any age? children *of*
any age?

OLD MAN: [*to* MRS LOVELY] That's exactly what saved me:
the inner life, a quiet home, austerity, my scientific
research, philosophy, my message . . .

OLD WOMAN: [*to the* PHOTOGRAPHER] I've never been un-
faithful to my husband the General . . . not so hard!
You'll have me on the floor . . . I'm only his poor old
mother! [*She starts sobbing.*] A grand, great, grand [*She
repulses him.*] great . . . mother. It's my conscience that's
protesting like this. For me, the branch of the apple-tree
is broken. You must ask someone else to show you the
way. I don't want to gather life's roses. . . .

OLD MAN: [*to* MRS LOVELY] . . . preoccupations of a nobler

kind . . . [*The* OLD COUPLE *lead* MRS LOVELY *and the* PHOTOGRAPHER *up to the other two invisible guests, and bid them sit down.*]

OLD COUPLE: [*to the* PHOTOGRAPHER *and* MRS LOVELY] Sit down, sit down, please. [*The* OLD PAIR *sit down, he on the left, she on the right, with the four empty chairs between them. A long scene that is almost silent, except for an occasional Yes or No. The* OLD COUPLE *are listening to what the invisible guests are saying.*]

OLD WOMAN: [*to the* PHOTOGRAPHER] We've had one son . . . still alive, of course . . . he went away . . . it's the usual story . . . a bit strange perhaps . . . he left his parents . . . had a heart of gold . . . a very long time ago . . . And we loved him so much . . . he slammed the door. . . . My husband and I struggled with him to try and stop him going . . . he was seven years old, the age of discretion. We called after him: My son, my child, my son, my child . . . and he never looked round . . .

OLD MAN: No . . . no . . . I'm sorry to say we never had children . . . I should have liked a son . . . so would Semiramis . . . we did what we could . . . poor Semiramis, she's such a motherly woman. Perhaps it was better that way. I myself was an ungrateful child . . . Oh dear! . . . Grief, regrets and remorse, that's all there is . . . all that's left . . .

OLD WOMAN: He used to say: You kill the birds! Why do you kill the birds? . . . We don't kill birds . . . we've never hurt a fly . . . His eyes were full of tears. He wouldn't let us wipe them away. He wouldn't let us near him. He would say: Yes, you do, you kill all the birds, all the birds . . . and he would wave his little fists at us . . . You're telling lies, you're trying to deceive me! The streets are full of the birds you've killed and the little

children dying. Can't you hear the birds singing? . . .
No, I can only hear moaning and groaning. The sky is
red with blood . . . No, my child, the sky is blue . . .
And again he would cry: You've deceived me, and I
loved you so much, I thought you were good . . . the
streets are full of dead birds, you've put out their eyes . . .
Daddy, mummy, you're wicked, wicked! . . . I won't
stay with you any more . . . I threw myself at his feet . . .
His father was weeping. But we couldn't hold him back
We could still hear him shouting: It's all your fault . . .
but what does that mean?

OLD MAN: I left my mother to die all alone in a ditch. She
called after me, crying feebly: My little boy, my beloved
child, don't leave me to die all alone . . . Stay with me.
I'm not long for this world. Don't worry, mother, I said,
I'll soon be back. I was in a hurry . . . I was going to a
dance. I'll be back soon. When I did come back, she was
dead and buried deep in the ground. I started digging to
try and find her . . . but I couldn't. . . . I know, I know it
always happens, sons leaving their mothers and as good
as killing their fathers . . . Life is like that. . . . but it tortures me . . . the others don't mind . . .

OLD WOMAN: He shouted: Daddy, mummy, I shall never
see you again . . .

OLD MAN: It tortures me, yes, but not the others . . .

OLD WOMAN: Don't talk to my husband about him. *He* was
so fond of *his* parents. He never left them for a moment.
He looked after them, spoiled them even . . . They died in
his arms and these were their last words: You have been
a wonderful son to us, God will be kind to you.

OLD MAN: I can still see her lying in that ditch and in her
hand there was a lily of the valley, and she cried out:
Remember me, remember me . . . her eyes were full of

tears, and she called me by the nickname I had as a child: Little chick, she said, little chick, don't leave me here all alone.

OLD WOMAN: [*to the* PHOTOGRAPHER] He's never written to us. Now and again a friend tells us he's seen him here or there, that he's well, that he's made a good husband . . .

OLD MAN: [*to* MRS LOVELY] She'd been in her grave a long time, when I came back. [*To the first* LADY:] Oh, but there is, Madam! There's a cinema in the house, and a restaurant, and bathrooms . . .

OLD WOMAN: [*to the* COLONEL] Why, yes, Colonel, it's just because he . . .

OLD MAN: When you come to think of it, that's all it really is. [*A very broken conversation, slowly coming to a stop.*]

OLD WOMAN: If only!

OLD MAN: So I didn't . . . told him . . . Naturally . . .

OLD WOMAN: [*Dialogue completely disconnected, run right down*] Well . . .

OLD MAN: To ours and to theirs.

OLD WOMAN: To what.

OLD MAN: I to him.

OLD WOMAN: Him, or her?

OLD MAN: Them.

OLD WOMAN: Peppermints . . . You don't say.

OLD MAN: There aren't.

OLD WOMAN: Why?

OLD MAN: Yes.

OLD WOMAN: I.

OLD MAN: Well.

OLD WOMAN: Well.

OLD MAN: [*to the first* LADY] Beg pardon, Madam? [*A long silence, the old pair motionless on their chairs. Then the bell rings again.*]

OLD MAN: [*with an excitement that goes on increasing*] They're coming. People. More people.

OLD WOMAN: I thought I could hear some boats . . .

OLD MAN: I'll go and open the door. Fetch some chairs. Please excuse me ladies, and gentlemen. [*He moves towards Door No. 7.*]

OLD WOMAN: [*to the invisible guests who are already there*] Please stand up for a moment. The Orator should be coming soon. I must get the room ready for the lecture. [*The* OLD WOMAN *arranges the chairs, their backs towards the audience.*] Would you mind helping me? Thank you.

OLD MAN: [*opening Door No. 7*] Good evening, Ladies and Gentlemen. Will you kindly come in? Mind your heads! [*The three or four invisible people who arrive are very tall, and the* OLD MAN *has to stand on tiptoe to shake hands with them. The* OLD WOMAN *follows the* OLD MAN *when she has arranged the chairs as described above.*]

OLD MAN: [*introducing everyone*] My wife . . . Mr . . . Mrs . . . my wife . . . Mr . . . Mrs . . . my wife . . .

OLD WOMAN: Who are all these people so tall, my love?

OLD MAN: Because they're journalists. Go and fetch some chairs, dear.

OLD WOMAN: I can't see to everything! . . . [*She goes out, grumbling, through Door No. 7, while the* OLD MAN *brings out the new arrivals to the front of the stage.*]

OLD MAN: Mind you don't drop your cine-camera . . . [*More introductions:*] The Colonel . . . the Lady . . . Mrs Lovely . . . The Photographer . . . Here are the journalists, they've come to listen to the lecture too; he's sure to be here soon . . . Don't get impatient . . . you won't be bored . . . with all of you together . . . [*The* OLD WOMAN *makes her appearance through Door No. 7, carrying two chairs.*] Hurry up, there, a little quicker with those chairs . . . we need one more. [*The* OLD WOMAN *goes off, still grumbling, to look for another through Door No. 3 and comes back through Door No. 8.*]

OLD WOMAN: All right, all right... I'm doing my best... I'm not a machine... Who are all these people? [*She goes out.*]

OLD MAN: Please sit down, the ladies with the ladies, the gentlemen with the gentlemen, or the other way around, if you prefer... We haven't any better chairs... we have to make do with what we have... so sorry... take the one in the middle... do you need a pen?... phone 'Maillot' and you'll get Monique... Claude is 'Providence'... I haven't got a wireless... Yes, I take all the newspapers... it depends on a number of things; I look after the lodgings, but I have no staff... have to economize, you know... *please*, no interviews, not just now... we'll see, afterwards... there'll be a seat for you in just a moment... but what can she be doing?... [*The* OLD WOMAN *appears through Door No. 8 with a chair.*] Faster, Semiramis...

OLD WOMAN: I'm doing my best... Who are all these people?

OLD MAN: I'll tell you later.

OLD WOMAN: And that girl, that tall thing, my love?

OLD MAN: Don't worry about her... [*To the* COLONEL:] Don't you think, Colonel, that journalism, as a profession, is rather like a warrior's?... [*To the* OLD WOMAN:] Look after the ladies, my dear... [*The bell rings. The* OLD MAN *rushes to Door No. 8.*] I'm coming, wait a minute... [*To the* OLD WOMAN:] What about those chairs!

OLD WOMAN: Forgive me, ladies and gentlemen, if I... [*She goes out through Door No. 3 to come back through Door No. 2; the* OLD MAN *goes to open the concealed door, Door No. 9, and disappears just as the* OLD WOMAN *comes back through Door No. 3.*]

OLD MAN: [*hidden from view*] Come in . . . come in . . . come in . . . come in . . . [*He reappears, leading in a large number of people, among them a very small child, whose hand he is holding.*] Nobody should bring a small child to a lecture on science . . . the poor little chap'll be bored to tears . . . it'll be a fine thing if he starts yelling and wets all the ladies' dresses! [*He leads them to the centre of the stage; the* OLD WOMAN *arrives with two chairs.*] May I introduce my wife, Semiramis, these are their children.

OLD WOMAN: Ladies, Gentlemen . . . Oh! Aren't they little dears!

OLD MAN: That one is the youngest.

OLD WOMAN: Isn't he sweet . . . sweet . . . really sweet!

OLD MAN: There aren't enough chairs.

OLD WOMAN: Oh dear oh dear oh dear oh dear . . . [*She goes out to find another chair; from now on she will go out and come in through Doors No. 2 and 3, on the right.*]

OLD MAN: Take the little one on your lap . . . the twins can use the same chair. Be careful, it's not a very strong one . . . these chairs belong to the house, they're the owner's. Yes, children, you're right, he'll be cross with us, he's a nasty old man. . . . He'd like us to buy them, but they're not worth the money. [*The* OLD WOMAN *comes up with another chair, as fast as she can.*] You don't all know each other, do you? . . . it's the first time you've met . . . but you used to know each other by name . . . [*To the* OLD WOMAN:] Semiramis, help me to introduce everyone . . .

OLD WOMAN: Who are all these people? . . . May I introduce—forgive me, may I introduce . . . but who are they?

OLD MAN: May I introduce you to . . . troduce you to . . . introduce you to her . . . Mr, Mrs, Miss . . . Mr . . . Mrs . . . Mrs . . . Mr . . .

OLD WOMAN: [*to the* OLD MAN] Did you put your pullover

on? [*To the invisible guests:*] Mr, Mrs, Mr . . . [*Bell rings again.*]

OLD MAN: More people! [*Bell rings again.*]

OLD WOMAN: More! [*Bell rings again, then again, and again. The* OLD MAN *is overwhelmed; the chairs, the backs turned to the audience so that they face the platform, are lined up in straight rows, as though arranged for a show, and grow more and more numerous; the* OLD MAN, *out of breath and mopping his brow, goes from one door to the next and seats the invisible people, while the* OLD WOMAN, *absolutely exhausted, clippity-clops as fast as she can from door to door, fetching and carrying chairs. There are now vast numbers of invisible people on the stage; the* OLD COUPLE *have to take care not to bump into them, and must pick their way through the rows of chairs. The movements could be arranged as follows: The* OLD MAN *goes to Door No. 4, the* OLD WOMAN *goes out through Door No. 3 and comes back through Door No. 2; the* OLD MAN *goes to open Door No. 7, the* OLD WOMAN *goes out through Door No. 8 and comes back through Door No. 6 with the chairs, etc., so that they go right round the stage, using all the doors.*]

OLD WOMAN: Excuse me . . . sorry . . . what . . . right . . . sorry . . . excuse me . . .

OLD MAN: Gentlemen . . . come in . . . Ladies . . . come in . . . it's you, Madam . . . allow me . . . yes. . . .

OLD WOMAN: [*with the chairs*] There . . . and there . . . too many people . . . there are really too many . . . too many, really, ah! there there there there. . . . [*From outside the noise of the boats on the water can be heard growing louder and nearer; all the noises off now come only from the wings. The* OLD COUPLE *go on executing the movements indicated above; doors are opened, chairs are brought in. The bell rings and rings.*]

OLD MAN: This table's in the way. [*He moves it, or rather he appears to be moving a table, in such a way as not to slow the action down, the* OLD WOMAN *helping him.*] There's hardly enough room here, please excuse us . . .

OLD WOMAN: [*as she pretends to be helping the* OLD MAN *to move the table*] Did you put your pullover on? [*Bell rings.*]

OLD MAN: More people! More chairs! People! Chairs! Come in, come in, Ladies, Gentlemen . . . Faster, Semiramis . . . I'd help you if I could . . .

OLD WOMAN: Excuse me . . . so sorry . . . good evening, Madam . . . Madam . . . Sir . . . Sir . . . yes, yes, the chairs . . .

OLD MAN: [*while the sound of the bell grows louder and louder and the noise of the boats bumping the landing-stage becomes more and more frequent, he gets tied up in the chairs, and has hardly enough time to go from one door to the other, for the bell is being rung almost continuously.*] Yes, straightaway . . . did you put your pullover on? Yes, yes . . . coming at once, be patient, yes, yes . . . patience . . .

OLD WOMAN: Your pullover? My pullover? . . . sorry, sorry.

OLD MAN: This way, Ladies, Gentlemen, this way, *please . . .* please . . . sorry . . . plea . . . come in . . . come in . . . I'll take you . . . there, the seats, my dear friend . . . not that way . . . be careful . . . you, a friend of mine! . . . [*Then, for some time, not a word: just the continuous sound of waves, boats and the bells being rung. The movement on the stage has reached a climax. All the doors now open and close ceaselessly. Only the large door at the back remains shut. The* OLD COUPLE *rush about from door to door, without saying a word; they look as though they are on roller-skates. The* OLD MAN *welcomes the guests, not accompanying them very far, just taking a few steps with them to show them where to sit; he has not time for more. The* OLD WOMAN *brings on chairs. Occasionally the* OLD

38

COUPLE *meet and collide, without interrupting the general move-ment. Then, back-centre of the stage, the* OLD MAN *starts turn-ing from left to right, right to left, etc., standing on the same spot and facing each door in turn: in the same way he points out seats to the guests, so quickly that his arm is whirling round at great speed. Similarly the* OLD WOMAN *stops, chair in hand, sets it down, picks it up and sets is down again; from left to right, from right to left, it looks as if she too wishes to go to each door in turn, but only her face and neck are moving, at great speed. None of this should hold up the movement of the scene, as the* OLD COUPLE *must give the impression, although standing in the same place, that they have not stopped rushing about: the quick little gestures, circular perhaps, that they make with their hands, torso, head and eyes should at last, very gradually begin to get slower; the bell-ringing not so loud, less frequent, the doors open less quickly. When finally the doors stop opening and shutting and there is no more bell-ringing, one should have the impression that the stage is overflowing with people.*]

OLD MAN: I'll find a place for you . . . don't worry . . . Semiramis, where the dickens . . .

OLD WOMAN: [*with a dramatic gesture; she is empty-handed*] There aren't any more chairs, my love. [*Then she suddenly starts selling invisible programmes in the crammed audi-torium, whose doors are all closed now.*] Programme! Pro-gramme! Would you like a programme, Sir? Programme, Madam?

OLD MAN: Don't get excited, Ladies and Gentlemen, you'll all be attended to . . . each one in turn, by order of arrival . . . there'll be room for you all. We'll manage somehow.

OLD WOMAN: Programme! Programme! Just a moment, Madam, please! I can't serve everybody at once, I haven't got thirteen pairs of hands, I'm not a cow, you

know . . . Sir, I wonder if you'd mind passing this programme to the lady next to you? Thank you . . . Change?
No, I haven't any . . .

OLD MAN: But I've told you we'll find you a seat! Don't get
in such a state! This way, it's this way, there, be careful
now . . . Oh! How nice to see you . . .

OLD WOMAN: Programme! Would you like . . . Programme
. . . gramme. . . .

OLD MAN: Yes, my boy, she's down there, a little further
down, selling programmes . . . no such thing as a stupid
job . . . that's her . . . seen her? . . . there's a seat for you
in the second row . . . on the right . . . no, on the left . . .
that's right! . . .

OLD WOMAN: . . . gramme . . . gramme . . . programme . . .
like a programme . . .

OLD MAN: Well, what else can I do? I'm doing my best!
[*To some invisible seated guests:*] Pull your chairs a little
closer together, please . . . a little more room there and
you can sit down, Madam . . . that's right. [*He is forced up
on the platform by the pressure of the crowd.*] Ladies, Gentlemen, I am very sorry to announce that now it's standing
room only . . .

OLD WOMAN: [*who is standing exactly opposite him, on the other
side of the stage between Door No. 3 and the window*] Programme, programme! . . . Would anyone like a programme? Choc ices, toffees . . . acid drops . . . [*Unable to
move an inch, she is so pressed in by the crowd she has to throw
her programmes and her sweets out at random over the heads of
the invisible guests.*] Here you are! there you are!

OLD MAN: [*standing on the platform, very excited; he is jostled
down from the platform, struggles up again, is forced down, hits
someone in the face and gets an elbow dug in his ribs; he says:*]
So sorry . . . Oh, I *am* sorry . . . do be careful . . . [*Knocked

off his balance, he has a job to keep his feet and clings onto someone's shoulders.]

OLD WOMAN: Who on earth are all these people? Programme, would you like a programme, choc ices?

OLD MAN: Ladies and Gentlemen, *please*! Silence for a moment, I beg you! . . . Quiet please! . . . an important announcement . . . all those who have not been able to find seats are kindly asked to leave the gangways clear . . . that's right . . . don't stand between the chairs.

OLD WOMAN: [*almost shouting to the* OLD MAN] Who are all these people, my pet? What are they all doing here?

OLD MAN: Move to one side, Ladies and Gentlemen. Those who have no seats must not stand in front of the others, but should line up along the walls there, on the right and the left . . . don't worry, you'll be able to see and hear everything, wherever you are! [*There is a general shift round; pushed by the crowd the* OLD MAN *will move almost round the stage to end up by the window on the right, near the stool; the* OLD WOMAN *will do the same, but in the opposite direction, to end up by the stool near the window on the left.*]

OLD MAN: [*as he carries out this movement*] Don't push so, don't push.

OLD WOMAN: [*as above*] Don't push so, don't push.

OLD MAN: [*as above*] Don't push, don't!

OLD WOMAN: [*as above*] Ladies, don't push. Don't push, Gentlemen.

OLD MAN: [*as above*] Don't get excited . . . there's no hurry . . . gently, please . . . what the . . .

OLD WOMAN: [*as before*] Anyone would think you were a lot of savages. [*At last they have arrived at their final positions, each one near a window: the* OLD MAN *on the left, by the window next to the platform, the* OLD WOMAN *on the right. They will not move again until the end.*]

OLD WOMAN: [*calling to the* OLD MAN] My pet . . . I can't
see you . . . where are you? Who are they? What do all
these people want? Who's that one?

OLD MAN: Where are you? Where are you, Semiramis?

OLD WOMAN: Where are you, my love?

OLD MAN: Here, next to the window . . . can you hear
me? . . .

OLD WOMAN: Yes, I can hear your voice! And a lot of
others, too, but I can pick yours out . . .

OLD MAN: And you, where are you?

OLD WOMAN: I'm at the window, too! . . . I feel frightened,
my love, there are too many people here . . . we're a long
way from each other . . . we ought to be careful, at our
age . . . we might get lost . . . we must keep together, you
never know, my love, my pet . . .

OLD MAN: Hallo! . . . I've just caught sight of you . . . oh!
. . . we'll be together again, don't worry . . . I'm with
some friends. [*To the friends:*] What a pleasure it is to
shake hands with you again. . . . But of course, I believe in
progress, steady progress, with set-backs obviously, and
yet, and yet . . .

OLD WOMAN: Quite well, thank you . . . What terrible
weather . . . How beautiful it's been! [*Aside.*] And yet
I'm still frightened . . . What am I doing here? . . .
[*Shouting.*] My love, my pet! . . . [*Each of them talks to the
guests separately.*]

OLD MAN: To prevent the exploitation of man by man, we
need money, money and still more money!

OLD WOMAN: My love! [*Then she is monopolized by friends.*]
Yes, my husband's here, it's he who did the organizing
. . . over there . . . Oh, you'll never reach him now . . .
you'd have to push your way through . . . he's standing
with friends . . .

OLD MAN: Of course not . . . that's what I've always said . . . there's no such thing as pure logic . . . it's just pretence.

OLD WOMAN: But you know there are some happy people. In the morning they breakfast in an aeroplane, they have their mid-day meal on a train and in the evening they dine at sea. They spend the night in lorries that go rumbling, rumbling, rumbling . . .

OLD MAN: You talk about the dignity of man? At least, let's try to save his face. Dignity's only his back.

OLD WOMAN: Don't fall down in the dark. [*She bursts out laughing during the conversation.*]

OLD MAN: That's what your compatriots ask me.

OLD WOMAN: Certainly . . . tell me all about it.

OLD MAN: I've called you all together . . . to have it explained to you . . . The person and the individual are one and the same person.

OLD WOMAN: There's something pinched about him. He's just out of prison for debt.

OLD MAN: I am not myself, I am someone else. I am the one in the other.

OLD WOMAN: Children, learn not to trust one another.

OLD MAN: Sometimes I wake up to find absolute silence around me. That's what I mean by the sphere. It's complete in itself. However, one has to be careful. The whole shape may suddenly disappear. There are holes it escapes through.

OLD WOMAN: Just ghosts, after all, nobodies, of no importance whatever. . . . My husband's duties are of supreme importance, quite sublime.

OLD MAN: I'm sorry to say I can't agree with you! . . . I'll let you know what I think about all this in time . . . I have nothing more to say just now! . . . It's the Orator—we're waiting for him at the moment—who'll answer for me, who'll explain to you exactly how we feel about every thing . . . he'll make it all clear . . . when? . . . when the right time comes . . . you won't have to wait long now . . .

OLD WOMAN: [*to her friends*] The sooner the better . . . But of course . . . [*Aside.*] There's no peace for us now. If only they'd all go away! Where is my little pet? I can't see him any more . . .

OLD MAN: [*to his friends*] Don't be so impatient. You'll hear what my message is. In a few minutes.

OLD WOMAN: [*aside*] Ah! . . . I can hear his voice! . . . [*To her friends:*] Do you realize my husband's always been misunderstood? His great moment has come at last.

OLD MAN: Listen! Experience of all kinds has deepened my knowledge of life and philosophy . . . I am not a selfish man: I want all mankind to reap the benefit.

OLD WOMAN: Ouch! You're treading on my toes . . . I've got chilblains!

OLD MAN: I have perfected my system in every detail. [*Aside.*] The Orator ought to have come by now! [*Aloud.*] I have suffered greatly.

OLD WOMAN: We have both suffered a great deal. [*Aside.*] The Orator ought to have come by now. It's time he arrived.

OLD MAN: Suffered greatly and learnt a great deal.

OLD WOMAN: [*like an echo*] Suffered greatly and learnt a great deal.

OLD MAN: My system is perfect, you'll see for yourself.

OLD WOMAN: [*like an echo*] His system is perfect. You'll see for yourself.

OLD MAN: If only you are willing to follow my instructions.

OLD WOMAN: [*echo*] If only you'll follow his instructions.

OLD MAN: We must save the world! . . .

OLD WOMAN: [*echo*] Save his own soul by saving the world! . . .

OLD MAN: One truth for all men!

OLD WOMAN: [*echo*] One truth for all men!

OLD MAN: Do as I say!

OLD WOMAN: [*echo*] Do as he says!

OLD MAN: Because there's not a single doubt in my mind! . . .

OLD WOMAN: [*echo*] Not a single doubt in his mind!

OLD MAN: *Never* . . .

OLD WOMAN: [*echo*] Never, as long as you live . . . [*A great noise and a fanfare of trumpets are heard from the wings.*]

OLD WOMAN: What's happening? [*The noise increases; then the door at the back opens wide, with a crash. Through the open door there is nothing to be seen, but a strong light floods the stage, coming through the big door and the windows, which are also brilliantly lit, as the* EMPEROR *arrives.*]

OLD MAN: I don't know . . . it can't be . . . it's not possible . . . but yes . . . it's incredible . . . and yet . . . yes . . . why yes . . . yes . . . it's the Emperor! His Majesty the Emperor! [*The light reaches its maximum intensity, flooding through the open door and the windows; but it is a cold, empty light; there is more noise, which stops abruptly.*]

OLD WOMAN: My love, my love . . . who is it?

OLD MAN: Stand up! . . . it's His Majesty the Emperor! The Emperor, in my house, in our house . . . Semiramis . . . do you realize?

OLD WOMAN: [*not understanding*] The Emperor . . . the Emperor, my love? [*Then, suddenly she realizes.*] Ah yes! The Emperor! Your Majesty! Your Majesty! [*She starts crutseying wildly, grotesquely, a fantastic number of times.*] In our house! In our house!

OLD MAN: [*weeping with emotion*] Your Majesty!... Oh! My Emperor! My great, my little Emperor!... Oh! What a tremendous ... like a glorious dream ...

OLD WOMAN: [*like an echo*] Glorious dream ... glorious ...

OLD MAN: [*to the invisible crowd*] Ladies and Gentlemen! Rise to your feet! Our well-beloved Sovereign, our Emperor is among us! Hoorah! Hooray! [*He gets up on the stool and stands on tip-toe to catch a glimpse of the Emperor: the* OLD WOMAN *does the same on her side of the stage.*]

OLD WOMAN: Hoorah! Hooray! [*Stamping of feet.*]

OLD MAN: Your Majesty!... I'm here!... Your Majesty! Can you hear me? Can you see me? Well, tell His Majesty I'm here! Majesty! Majesty!!! I'm here, your most faithful servant!...

OLD WOMAN: [*still as echo*] Your most faithful servant, Majesty!

OLD MAN: Your servant, your slave, your faithful hound, aouh! aouh! your hound, Majesty ...

OLD WOMAN: [*baying loudly, like a hound*] Aouh ... aouh ... aouh ...

OLD MAN: [*wringing his hands*] Can you see me? Oh, answer me, Sire!... Ah, I can see you, I've just caught a glimpse of your Majesty's imperial countenance ... that brow divine ... I have seen it, yes, in spite of the courtiers who screen you from view ...

OLD WOMAN: In spite of the courtiers ... we are here, Majesty.

OLD MAN: Majesty! Majesty! Ladies and Gentlemen, you can't let His Majesty remain standing ... you see, my Majesty, I'm really the only one who looks after you, who worries about your health, I am the most loyal of all your subjects ...

OLD WOMAN: [*echo*] We're your most loyal subjects!

OLD MAN: Well, let me get down, Ladies and Gentlemen . . . how can I push my way through such a mob? . . . But I must go and pay my humble respects to His Majesty the Emperor. . . . Let me get down . . .

OLD WOMAN: [*echo*] Let him get down . . . let him get through . . .

OLD MAN: Let me through, let me get past then. [*Desperately.*] Oh! Shall I ever reach him?

OLD WOMAN: [*echo*] Reach him . . . reach him . . .

OLD MAN: But I still lay my heart and my whole being at his feet; there's such a crowd of courtiers round him, oh dear, oh dear, they want to keep me from him . . . they've a shrewd suspicion, all of them, that I'd . . . Oh! I know them! . . . I know all about Court intrigue . . . they want to keep me from Your Majesty.

OLD WOMAN: Don't upset yourself, my love . . . His Majesty can see you, he's looking at you . . . His Majesty just winked at me . . . His Majesty is on our side! . . .

OLD MAN: The best seat for His Majesty! . . . near the platform . . . so he can hear all the Orator says.

OLD WOMAN: [*hoisting herself up on her stool and standing on tiptoe, craning her neck up as high as she can, to have a better view*] Someone's looking after the Emperor at last.

OLD MAN: Thank Heaven for that! [*To the* EMPEROR:] Sire . . . Your Majesty can trust that man, he's a friend of mine, he's acting for me. [*Standing on the stool, on tip-toe.*] Ladies and Gentlemen, Children, little children, I implore you . . .

OLD WOMAN: [*echo*] Plore . . . plore . . .

OLD MAN: . . . I want to see . . . move aside . . . I want . . . that heavenly gaze, that imposing face, the crown, His Majesty's radiance . . . Sire, be pleased to turn your illustrious countenance towards your humble servant . . . so

47

very humble . . . oh! This time I can see quite clearly . . . I can see . . .

OLD WOMAN: [*echo*] He can see this time . . . he can . . . he can see-ee-ee . . .

OLD MAN: This is the height of happiness . . . I have no words to express the exceeding measure of my gratitude . . . in my simple dwelling, oh! Majesty! oh! Blazing sun! . . . here . . . here . . . in this building where I am, it's true, a General . . . though in the ranks of your army, I am just an ordinary Quartermaster . . .

OLD WOMAN: [*echo*] Quartermaster . . .

OLD MAN: I feel proud, proud and humble at the same time . . . that's just as it should be . . . alas! I'm a General, I know, but I could have been at the Imperial Court, here my court is a small backyard . . . Majesty . . . I . . . Majesty, I don't express myself very well . . . I could have had . . . a number of things, possessed quite a lot of good things in life, if I'd only known, if I'd wanted to, if I . . . if we . . . My Majesty, forgive my emotion . . .

OLD WOMAN: The third person, you must use the third person!

OLD MAN: [*maudlin*] May His Majesty condescend to forgive me! But you've come all the same . . . we'd given up hoping . . . we mightn't have been at home . . . oh! saviour, in my life I have suffered humiliation . . .

OLD WOMAN: [*echo, sobbing*] . . . milia . . . milia . . .

OLD MAN: My life has been full of suffering. . . . I could really have *been* someone, if only I could have counted on Your Majesty's support. . . . I have no one behind me . . . it would all have been too late, if you hadn't come . . . you are, Sire, my last hope in life . . .

OLD WOMAN: [*echo*] Last hopeinlife . . . Sire . . . opeinlife . . . p'inlife . . .

OLD MAN: I have brought ill-luck to my friends, to all those who have helped me . . . The lightning struck the outstretched hand . . .

OLD WOMAN: . . . stretched hand . . . retched hand . . . etched hand . . .

OLD MAN: I have always been hated for the right reasons, and loved for the wrong ones . . .

OLD WOMAN: That's not true, my pet, not true. You've got me to love you, to be your little mother . . .

OLD MAN: All my enemies have been rewarded and my tried friends have betrayed me . . .

OLD WOMAN: [*echo*] Tried . . . trayed . . . trayed . . .

OLD MAN: They've wronged me and persecuted me. And if I complained, it was always *they* were proved right. . . . Sometimes I tried to revenge myself . . . I could never, never do it. . . . I had too much pity to lay the enemy low. . . . I've always been too good.

OLD WOMAN: [*echo*] He was too good, good, good, good, good . . .

OLD MAN: Pity was my undoing.

OLD WOMAN: [*echo*] Pity . . . pity . . . pity . . .

OLD MAN: But *they* had no pity. I would prick them with a pin; they'd attack me with their bludgeons, their knives and their cannon, and mangle my bones . . .

OLD WOMAN: [*echo*] . . . bones . . . bones . . . bones.

OLD MAN: I was robbed of my positions, my possessions, my life . . . I was a collector of disasters, a lightning conductor for catastrophe . . .

OLD WOMAN: [*echo*] Conductor . . . catastrophe . . . astrophe . . .

OLD MAN: In order to forget, Majesty, I tried to take up sport . . . mountaineering . . . my feet were pulled from under me . . . when I tried to climb the stairs, I found the

49

wood was rotten . . . and the staircase collapsed . . . when I wanted to travel, I was refused a passport . . . when I wanted to cross the river, the bridges were blown . . .

OLD WOMAN: [*echo*] Bridges were blown.

OLD MAN: I tried to cross the Pyrenees, but the Pyrenees had gone.

OLD WOMAN: [*echo*] Pyrenees had gone . . . he too, Majesty, like so many others, could have been a General Editor, a Director-General, a General Physician, Majesty or a Generalissimo . . .

OLD MAN: And then, no one ever took any notice of me . . . nobody ever sent me invitations . . . and yet it was I, I tell you, it was I and I alone who could have saved mankind, suffering, sick mankind. Your Majesty understands this, as I do . . . or at least I could have spared men the ills they have endured in the last twenty-five years, if only I had had the chance to pass on my message; I haven't given up hope of saving mankind, there is still time, and my plan is ready . . . but I find it so difficult to express myself . . .

OLD WOMAN: [*shouting above the invisible heads*] The Orator will be here, he'll speak for you . . . His Majesty is here . . . so they'll listen to him, you needn't worry any more, you're holding all the trumps, it's not the same now, it's all different . . .

OLD MAN: May Your Majesty forgive me . . . with so many cares of State . . . I have been humiliated . . . Ladies and Gentlemen, move aside just a little, don't stand right under his Majesty's nose, I want to see the diamonds blazing in the Imperial Crown . . . But if Your Majesty has been pleased to enter my poor dwelling, it must be because he deigns to show some regard for my unworthy self. What a wonderful recompense. Majesty, if physically speaking I am stretching up on the tips of my toes, it is not out of pride, but simply to behold your face! . . . morally speaking, I am down on my knees before you . . .

OLD WOMAN: [*sobbing*] At your knees, Sire, we are at your knees, at your feet, at your toes . . .

OLD MAN: I once had scabies, Sire. My employer gave me the sack, because I would not bow down to his baby and his horse. I have been kicked in the backside, but none of that's important now, Sire . . . because . . . because . . . Majesty . . . look at me . . . I am here . . . here . . .

OLD WOMAN: [*echo*] Here . . . here . . . here . . . here . . . here . . . here . . .

OLD MAN: Because Your Majesty is here . . . because Your Majesty will heed my message . . . But the Orator should be here . . . He is keeping His Majesty waiting . . .

OLD WOMAN: I beg Your Majesty to forgive him. He should be coming now. He'll be here in a moment. We've just had a telephone call.

OLD MAN: His Majesty is most kind. His Majesty would never leave without having heard a word, he will stay, to hear everything.

OLD WOMAN: [*echo*] Heard a word . . . hear everything . . .

OLD MAN: It is he who will speak in my name . . . I'm afraid I can't . . . I haven't the gift . . . *he* has all the papers, all the documents . . .

OLD WOMAN: [*echo*] He has all the documents . . .

OLD MAN: A little patience, Sire, I beg you . . . he is just coming.

OLD WOMAN: He'll be here in a moment.

OLD MAN: [*so that the* EMPEROR *shall not grow impatient*] Let me tell you, Majesty, how the revelation came to me a very long time ago . . . I was forty years old . . . I'm saying this for you, too, Ladies and Gentlemen . . . one day, after

51

the evening meal, I was sitting on my father's lap, as usual, before I went to bed . . . my moustache was bigger than his, and more pointed . . . my chest more hairy . . . my hair already turning grey, his was still brown . . . We had some visitors, grown-up people, at table and they started laughing, laughing.

OLD WOMAN: [*echo*] Laughing . . . laughing . . .

OLD MAN: This isn't a joke, I told them. I'm fond of my daddy. And they replied: It's midnight, and a youngster doesn't stay up so late. If you've not gone to bed yet, it's because you're a man, don't forget. I wouldn't have believed a word they said, if they hadn't talked about going to bed . . .

OLD WOMAN: [*echo*] Bed.

OLD MAN: Instead of going bye-byes . . .

OLD WOMAN: Bye-byes . . .

OLD MAN: And then I thought: But I'm not married yet. So I must still be a child. And they married me off on the spot, just to prove I was wrong. . . . Luckily my wife has been a mother and a father to me . . .

OLD WOMAN: The Orator should be here now, Majesty . . .

OLD MAN: Just coming, the Orator.

OLD WOMAN: Just coming.

OLD MAN: Just coming.

OLD WOMAN: Just coming.

OLD MAN: Just coming.

OLD WOMAN: Just coming.

OLD MAN: Just coming, just coming.

OLD WOMAN: Just coming, just coming.

OLD MAN: Coming.

OLD WOMAN: Coming.

OLD MAN: Coming.

OLD WOMAN: Coming, he's here.

OLD MAN: Coming, he's here.

OLD WOMAN: Coming, he's here.

BOTH: He's here . . .

OLD MAN: Here he is! . . . [*Silence. Not a movement. Turned to stone, the* OLD COUPLE *have their eyes fixed on Door No. 5; the stage remains quite still for a considerable time, about half a minute; then the door opens wide, silently and very, very slowly. The* ORATOR *appears: a real person. He looks like the typical painter or poet of the last century: a wide-brimmed black felt hat, a loosely tied cravat, an artist's jacket, moustache and goatee beard, rather a smug-pretentious look about him. If the invisible characters should appear as real as possible, the* ORATOR *should look unreal; slipping along the right-hand wall, he goes quietly to the back of the stage, in front of the great door, without moving his head to right or left; he passes close to the* OLD WOMAN *without seeming to notice her, even when she touches his arm to make sure he is really there; it is at this point that the* OLD WOMAN *says:*] Here he is!

OLD MAN: Here he is!

OLD WOMAN: [*who has been following him with her eyes, and goes on doing so*] He's here all right, he really exists. In flesh and blood.

OLD MAN: [*watching him, too*] He exists. And he's here all right. It's not a dream!

OLD WOMAN: It's not a dream, I told you it wasn't. [*The* OLD MAN *clasps his hands and raises his eyes to Heaven; he is exulting, silently. When the* ORATOR *has reached the back of the stage, he removes his hat and bows in silence; he greets the invisible* EMPEROR *with a flourish of his hat, like one of the Musketeers and a little like a robot. Then:*]

OLD MAN: Majesty . . . may I present the Orator . . .

OLD WOMAN: That's him! [*Then the* ORATOR *puts his hat on again and mounts the platform. From there he looks down, over the heads of his invisible public, at the chairs; he freezes into a solemn pose.*]

OLD MAN: [*to the invisible public*] You may ask for his auto-graph. [*Silently, autmoatically, the* ORATOR *signs and gives out countless autographs. Meanwhile the* OLD MAN *clasps his hands and raises his eyes again to Heaven in exultation:*] No man on earth can ask more of life . . .

OLD WOMAN: [*echo*] No man can ask for more.

OLD MAN: [*to the invisible crowd*] And now, with Your Majesty's permission, I should like to speak to you all, Ladies and Gentlemen, young children, my dear col-leagues and fellow-countrymen all, Mr Chairman, com-rades in arms . . .

OLD WOMAN: [*echo*] Children in arms . . . arms . . . arms . . .

OLD MAN: Speak to you all, without distinction of age, sex, civil status or social rank, of trade or profession, in order to thank you, from the bottom of my heart . . .

OLD WOMAN: [*echo*] Thank you . . .

OLD MAN: As I would thank the Orator, most warmly, for coming here in such great numbers . . . Silence, Gentle-men! . . .

OLD WOMAN: [*echo*] Silence, Gentlemen . . .

OLD MAN: I should also like to thank all those who have made this meeting possible tonight, the organizers . . .

OLD WOMAN: Hear! Hear! [*Meanwhile, on the platform, the* ORATOR *is solemn and motionless, except for his hand, which goes on automatically signing autographs.*]

OLD MAN: The owners of this building, the architect, and the masons who were kind enough to raise these walls! . . .

OLD WOMAN: [*echo*] . . . walls . . .

OLD MAN: All those who dug the foundations . . . Silence, Ladies and Gentlemen . . .

OLD WOMAN: [*echo*] . . . dies and Gentlemen . . .

OLD MAN: I wish to give particular thanks—for I am not forgetting them—to the joiners who made the chairs you're sitting on, to the skilful craftsman . . .

OLD WOMAN: [*echo*] . . . ilful . . . aftsman . . .

OLD MAN: . . . who fashioned the armchair, in which Your Majesty so softly nestles, his mind still sharp and keen . . . Thanks again to all the technicians, mechanics, electocutioners . . .

OLD WOMAN: [*echo*] . . . cutioners . . . cutioners . . .

OLD MAN: . . . paper manufacturers and printers, proof-readers and editors, to whom we owe the programmes, so attractively designed, I give thanks to the universal solidarity of the human race, thanks to our country, thanks to the State [*He turns in the direction of the* EMPEROR.] whose ship Your Majesty guides with the skill and know-ledge of a true helmsman . . . thanks to the happy programme-seller . . .

OLD WOMAN: [*echo*] hapigram hapigram . . .

OLD MAN: [*pointing to the* OLD WOMAN] . . . for her sweets and ices . . .

OLD WOMAN: [*echo*] . . . sand-ices . . .

OLD MAN: . . . my wife and comrade . . . Semiramis! . . .

OLD WOMAN: [*echo*] . . . ife . . . com . . . miss . . . [*Aside.*] Bless his heart, he never forgets to mention me.

OLD MAN: I should like to thank all those who, by their financial or moral encouragement, valuable and efficient support, have thus contributed to the phenomenal success of our celebration this evening . . . thanks once more, and above all, to our well-loved Sovereign, His Majesty the Emperor . . .

OLD WOMAN: [*echo*] . . . jesty th' Emperor . . .

OLD MAN: [*in complete silence*] . . . Quiet, please . . . Majesty . . .

OLD WOMEN: [*echo*] . . . ajesty . . . jesty . . .

OLD MAN: Majesty, my wife and myself have nothing more to ask of life. Our existence has found its final consummation . . . Thanks be to Heaven that we have been granted so many long and peaceful years . . . My life has been a full one. My mission is accomplished. I shall not have lived in vain, since my message is to be revealed to the world . . . [*With a gesture to the* ORATOR, *who does not notice it: he is busy rejecting requests for autographs with a firm and dignified wave of the arm.*] To the world, or rather to what is left of it! [*Broad gesture to take in the invisible crowd.*] To *you*, Ladies and Gentlemen, my dear friends, the left-over scraps of humanity, from which good soup can still be made . . . My friend, the Orator . . . [*The* ORATOR *is looking somewhere else.*] If I have been misrepresented and misunderstood by my contemporaries for a long time now, it must have been ordained so . . . [*The* OLD WOMAN *sobs.*] But what does all that matter now I can leave to you, dear friend and Orator [*The* ORATOR *repulses a fresh demand for an autograph; then strikes an attitude expressing indifference and gazes round on all sides.*] . . . the task of dazzling posterity with the enlightenment I bring . . . So make my philosophy known to the Universe. And do not omit the details of my private life, whether they're comical, painful or touching, my habits and tastes, my gorgeous greed . . . tell all you know . . . speak of my dear companion [*The* OLD WOMAN *sobs still louder.*] . . . of the way she used to prepare those marvellous little Turkish pasties of hers, and her rabbit *rillettes à la normandillette* . . . talk about Berry, where I was born . . . I am looking to you, Master Orator . . . as for me and my faithful spouse, after long years of labour in the cause of human progress, years in which we have fought for what is right and just, it only remains for us to withdraw from the scene . . . and at once, in order to make the supreme sacrifice: no one demands it of us, nevertheless we are resolved . . .

OLD WOMAN: [*sobbing*] Yes, yes, let us die in our moment of glory . . . so that our names become legendary . . . at least we shall have a street called after us . . .

OLD MAN: [*to the* OLD WOMAN] Oh! My faithful wife and companion! . . . you who have believed in me, without a moment's doubt, for a whole century, who have never left my side, never . . . today, alas, in our moment of triumph, we are separated by a pitiless mob . . .

> And yet I would
> Have found it good
> That you and I
> As one might lie
> Each bone to bone
> Beneath one stone
> Our old flesh breeding
> The same worms feeding
> Mouldering together . . .

OLD WOMAN: . . . mouldering together.

OLD MAN: Alas! . . . Alack! . . .

OLD WOMAN: Alas! . . . Alack! . . .

OLD MAN: . . . Our bodies will fall far from one another, we shall rot in watery solitude . . . Let us not complain too much.

OLD WOMAN: We must do what must be done! . . .

OLD MAN: We shall not be forgotten. The eternal Emperor will always remember us, always.

OLD WOMAN: [*echo*] Always.

OLD MAN: We shall leave some trace behind, for we are not towns, but people.

BOTH: [*together*] A street will bear our names!

OLD MAN: Let us be united in time and eternity, if not in space, as we were in trial and tribulation; let us die at the same moment . . . [*To the impassive, motionless* ORATOR:] Once more, then . . . I am depending on you . . . You must tell everything. . . . Bequeath the message to everyone . . . [*to the* EMPEROR:] With Your Majesty's permission . . . Farewell, to all of you. Farewell, Semiramis.

OLD WOMAN: Farewell, to all of you! . . . Farewell, my love!

OLD MAN: Long live the Emperor! [*He throws confetti and paper streamers over the invisible* EMPEROR; *a fanfare of trumpets is heard; a brilliant light, as from a firework.*]

OLD WOMAN: Long live the Emperor! [*Confetti and paper streamers over the* EMPEROR, *then over the impassive, motionless* ORATOR, *and over the empty chairs.*]

OLD MAN: [*more confetti, etc.*] Long live the Emperor!

OLD WOMAN: [*more confetti, etc.*] Long live the Emperor!

THE OLD COUPLE *at one and the same time both jump through their windows, crying 'Long live the Emperor!' A sudden silence; the firework's glares has gone, an 'Ah!' is heard from both sides of the stage, and the glaucous sound of bodies striking water. The light is no longer coming through the great door and the windows: there is only the dim light there was at the beginning; the wide-open windows gape black, the curtains flapping in the wind.*

THE ORATOR, *who has remained motionless and impassive during the scene of the double suicide, decides after a few moments' effort to speak; as he faces the rows of empty chairs, he indicates to the invisible crowd that he is deaf and dumb; he uses sign-language: desperate efforts to make himself understood; then from his throat come moans and groans and the sort of guttural sounds made by deaf mutes.*

He, Mme, mm, mm.

Ju, gou, hou, hou.

Heu, heu, gu, gou, gueu.

Helpless, his arms drop to his sides; suddenly his face lights up, he has an idea: he turns to the blackboard, takes a piece of chalk from his pocket, and writes in large capitals:

ANGELBREAD[1]

then:

NNAA NNM NWNWNW V

He turns again to his invisible public, the public on the stage, and points to what he has written on the blackboard.

ORATOR: Mmm, Mmm, Gueu, Gou, Gu, Mmm, Mmm, Mmm, Mmm. *Then, dissatisfied, he rubs out the chalk-marks with a series of sharp movements, and puts others in their place: among them the following can be discerned, in large capitals:*

ΛΑDIEU ΛDIEU ΛPΛ

Again the ORATOR *turns to the audience and smiles questioningly, as though he hopes he has been understood, has really said something; he points out to the empty chairs what he has just written; he waits, quite still, for a moment, looking fairly pleased and a little solemn; then, gradually, when the hoped-for reaction is not forthcoming, his smile disappears and his face clouds over; he waits a moment longer; then, suddenly, he bows moodily, abruptly, and comes down from the platform; he makes for the great door at the back with his ghostly walk; before he goes out through this door, he bows once more, ceremoniously, to the empty chairs and the invisible Emperor. The stage is empty, apart from the chairs, the platform, and the confetti and paper streamers over the floor. The door at the back is wide open, gaping black.*

For the first time human noises seem to be coming from the invisible crowd: snatches of laughter, whisperings, a 'Ssh!' or two, little sarcastic coughs; these noises grow louder and louder,

[1] Translator's Note: ANGEPAIN in the original.

only to start fading away again. All this should last just long enough for the real and visible public to go away with this ending firmly fixed in their minds. The curtain falls very slowly.[1]

CURTAIN

[1] When first produced, the curtain fell during the moaning of the dumb Orator. The blackboard was omitted.

THE KILLER

TRANSLATOR'S NOTE

An attempt has been made to reach a compromise between American and British English, but in the event of production, producers should feel themselves free to change any word that would obviously offend an audience.

Two cases in point would be: elevator/lift and prefect/monitor.

THE KILLER

First produced in Paris by José Quaglio at the Théâtre Récamier, the 27th February, 1959.

CHARACTERS, VOICES, SILHOUETTES
(in order of appearance):

    BÉRENGER, an average, middle-aged citizen.

    THE ARCHITECT, of ageless, bureaucratic age.

    DANY, young typist, conventional pin-up.

    THE CLOCHARD, drunk.

    THE OWNER OF THE BISTRO, middle-aged, fat, dark and hairy.

    ÉDOUARD, 35, thin, nervous, darkly dressed, in mourning.

    THE CONCIERGE (preceded by THE VOICE OF THE CONCIERGE), typical concierge.

    VOICE OF THE CONCIERGE'S DOG.

    A MAN'S VOICE.

    SECOND MAN'S VOICE.

    TRUCK DRIVER'S VOICE.

    CAR DRIVER'S VOICE.

    FIRST OLD MAN.

    SECOND OLD MAN.

    THE GROCER.

    SCHOOLMASTER'S VOICE.

    FIRST VOICE FROM THE STREET.

    SECOND VOICE (GRUFF) FROM THE STREET.

    THIRD VOICE (PIPING) FROM THE STREET.

    FOURTH VOICE FROM THE STERET.

    FIRST VOICE FROM BELOW.

Second Voice from Below.

Voice from the Right.

Voice from Above.

Voice from the Left.

Second Voice from the Left

Woman's Voice from the Entrance.

Silhouette of a Motorcyclist on his Bicycle.

Postman's Voice (preceding the Postman himself, if desired.)

Mother Peep.

Voices of the Crowd.

The Drunk in Top Hat and Tails.

The Old Gentleman with the Little White Beard.

First Policeman.

Second Policeman.

The Echo.

The Killer.

STAGE DIRECTIONS

Several of these parts may be played by the same actors. Moreover, it is probable that all the voices in the second act will not be heard. Any cuts required may be made in the first half of Act II: it will all depend on the effectiveness of these voices and their absurd remarks. The director can choose those he likes. He should, however, try if possible to obtain stereophonic sound effects. In the second act it is also better to have the greatest possible number of figures appearing in silhouette the other side of the window, as on a stage behind the stage. In any case, after the curtain has risen on the second act, some voices and sounds around the empty stage are indispensable, at least for a few minutes, in order to continue and in a way intensify the visual and aural atmosphere of street and city; this is first created at the end of Act I, fades after the arrival of Bérenger and returns again in force at the start of Act III to die right away at the end.

A few cuts could also be made in Act I, according to the power of the actor playing the part and his natural capacity to 'put it over'.

Berenger's speech to the Killer at the end of the play is one short act in itself. The text should be interpreted in such a way as to bring out the gradual breaking-down of Bérenger, his falling apart and the vacuity of his own rather commonplace morality, which collapses like a leaking balloon. In fact Bérenger finds within himself, in spite of himself and against his own will, arguments in favour of the Killer.

ACT ONE

No décor. An empty stage when the curtain rises. Later there will only be, on the left of the stage, two garden chairs and a table, which the ARCHITECT *will bring on himself. They should be near at hand in the wings.*

The atmosphere for Act I will be created by the lighting only. At first, while the stage is still empty, the light is grey, like a dull November day or afternoon in February. The faint sound of wind; perhaps you can see a dead leaf fluttering across the stage. In the distance the noise of a tram, vague outlines of houses; then, suddenly, the stage is brilliantly lit; a very bright, very white light; just this whiteness, and also the dense vivid blue of the sky. And so, after the grisaille, *the lighting effects should simply be made up of white and blue, the only elements in the décor. The noise of the tram, the wind and the rain will have stopped at the very moment the light changes. The blue, the white, the silence and the empty stage should give a strange impression of peace. The audience must be given time to become aware of this. Not until a full minute has passed should the characters appear on the scene.*

BÉRENGER *comes on first, from the left, moving quickly. He stops in the centre of the stage and turns round briskly to face the* ARCHITECT, *who has followed him more slowly.* BÉRENGER *is wearing a grey overcoat, hat and scarf. The* ARCHITECT *is in a summer-weight jacket, light trousers, open-necked shirt and without a hat; under his arm he is carrying a briefcase, rather thick and heavy, like the one* ÉDOUARD *has in Act* II.

BÉRENGER: Amazing! Amazing! It's extraordinary! As far as I can see, it's a miracle . . . [*Vague gesture of protest from the* ARCHITECT.] . . . A miracle, or, as I don't suppose you're a religious man, you'd rather I called it a marvel! I congratulate you most warmly, it's a marvel, really quite marvellous, you're a marvellous architect! . . .

ARCHITECT: Oh . . . you're very kind . . .

BÉRENGER: No, no. I *want* to congratulate you. It's absolutely incredible, you've achieved the incredible! The real thing is quite beyond imagination.

ARCHITECT: It's the work I'm commissioned to do, part of my normal duties, what I specialize in.

BÉRENGER: Why, yes, of course, to be sure, you're an architect, a technician and a conscientious civil servant at one and the same time . . . Still, that doesn't explain everything. [*Looking round him and staring at several fixed points on the stage*:] Beautiful, what a magnificent lawn, that flower-bed! . . . Oh, what flowers, appetizing as vegetables, and

66

what vegetables, fragrant as flowers . . . and what a blue
sky, what an amazingly blue sky. How wonderful it is!
[*To the* ARCHITECT:] In all the cities of the world, all cities
of a certain size, I'm sure there are civil servants, municipal architects like you, with the same duties as you, earn-
ing the same salary. But they're nowhere near achieving
the same results. [*Gesture of the hand.*] Are you well paid?
I'm sorry, perhaps I'm being indiscreet . . .

ARCHITECT: Please don't apologize . . . I'm fairly well
paid, the scale is laid down. It's reasonable . . . It's
all right.

BÉRENGER: But ingenuity like yours is worth its weight in
gold. And what's more, I mean the price gold fetched before 1914 . . . the real thing.

ARCHITECT: [*with a modestly disclaiming gesture*] Oh . . .

BÉRENGER: Oh yes it is . . . You're the town architect,
aren't you? . . . *Real* gold . . . After all, today, gold
has been devalued, like so many other things, it's paper
gold . . .

ARCHITECT: Your surprise, your . . .

BÉRENGER: Call it my admiration, my enthusiasm!

ARCHITECT: Very well, your enthusiasm, then, touches me
very deeply. I feel I must thank you, dear Monsieur . . .
Bérenger. [*The* ARCHITECT *bows in thanks, after first searching one of his pockets for a card which doubtless bears the name
of* BÉRENGER, *and as he bows he reads the name off the card.*]

BÉRENGER: Genuinely enthusiastic, quite genuinely. I'm not
the flattering kind, I can tell you.

ARCHITECT: [*ceremoniously, but unimpressed*] I am very highly
honoured.

BÉRENGER: It's magnificent! [*He looks about him.*] I'd been
told all about it, you see, but I didn't believe it . . . or
rather I wasn't told a thing about it, but I *knew* that some-

where in our dark and dismal city, in all its mournful, dusty, dirty districts, there was one that was bright and beautiful, this neighbourhood beyond compare, with its sunny streets and avenues bathed in light . . . this radiant city within a city which you've built . . .

ARCHITECT: It's a nucleus which is, or rather was, in theory meant to be extended. I planned it all by order of the City Council. I don't allow myself any personal initiative . . .

BÉRENGER: [*continuing his monologue*] I believed in it, without believing, I knew without knowing! I was afraid to hope . . . hope, that's not a French word any more, or Turkish, or Polish . . . Belgian perhaps . . . and even then . . .

ARCHITECT: I see, I understand.

BÉRENGER: And yet, *here* I am. Your radiant city is *real*. No doubt of that. You can touch it with your fingers. The blue brilliance of it looks absolutely natural . . . blue and green . . . oh, that grass, those rose-pink flowers . . .

ARCHITECT: Yes, those pink flowers really are roses.

BÉRENGER: Real roses? [*He walks about the stage, pointing, smelling the flowers, etc.*] More blue and more green things too . . . the colours of joy. And what peace, what peace!

ARCHITECT: That's the rule here, Monsieur . . . [*He reads off the card:*] . . . Bérenger. It's all calculated, all intentional. Nothing was to be left to chance in this district, the weather here is always fine. . . . And so the building plots always fetch . . . or rather . . . always used to fetch a high price . . . the villas are built of the best materials . . . built to last, built with care.

BÉRENGER: I don't suppose it ever rains in these houses?

ARCHITECT: Definitely not! That's the least you can expect. Does it rain in yours?

BÉRENGER: Yes, I'm afraid it does.

ARCHITECT: It oughtn't to, even in your district. I'll send a man round.

BÉRENGER: Well, I suppose it doesn't really rain *inside*. Only in a manner of speaking. It's so damp, it's as if it *was* raining.

ARCHITECT: I see. Morally speaking. In any case, here in this district it never rains at all. And yet all the walls and all the roofs of the buildings you can see are damp-proof. It's a habit, a matter of form. Quite unnecessary, but it keeps up an old tradition.

BÉRENGER: You say it *never* rains? And all these things growing? This grass? And not a dead leaf on the trees, not a faded flower in the garden!

ARCHITECT: They're watered from below.

BÉRENGER: A technical marvel! Forgive me for being so astonished, a layman like me . . . [*With his handkerchief he is mopping the sweat from his brow.*]

ARCHITECT: Why don't you take your overcoat off? Carry it on your arm, you're too hot.

BÉRENGER: Why yes . . . I'm not at all cold any more . . . Thank you, thanks for the suggestion. [*He takes off his over-coat and puts it over his arm; he keeps his hat on his head. He looks up, with a gesture:*] The leaves on the trees are small enough for the light to filter through, but not too big, so as not to darken the front of the houses. I must say it's amazing to think that in all the rest of the town the sky's as grey as the hair on an old woman's head, that there's dirty snow at the pavements' edge, and the wind blowing there. When I woke up this morning I was very cold. I was frozen. The radiators work so badly in my block of flats, especially on the ground-floor. They work even worse when they don't make up the fire . . . So I mean to say . . .

[*A telephone bell rings, coming from the* ARCHITECT's *pocket; the* ARCHITECT *takes a receiver from it and listens; the telephone wire ends in his pocket.*]

ARCHITECT: Hullo?

BÉRENGER: Forgive me, Monsieur, I'm keeping you from your work . . .

ARCHITECT: [*to telephone*] Hullo? [*To* BÉRENGER:] Not a bit . . . I've kept an hour free to show you the district. No trouble at all. [*To telephone:*] Hullo? Yes. I know about that. Let the assistant manager know. Right. Let him hold an investigation if he insists. *He* can make the official arrangements. I'm with Monsieur Bérenger, for the visit to the radiant city. [*He puts the machine back in his pocket. To* BÉRENGER, *who has taken a few steps away, lost in admiration:*] You were saying? Hey, where are you?

BÉRENGER: Here. I'm sorry. What was I saying? Oh yes . . . Oh, it doesn't really matter now.

ARCHITECT: Go ahead. Say it anyway.

BÉRENGER: I was saying . . . oh yes . . . in my district, especially where I live, everything is damp, the coal; the bread, the wind, the wine, the walls, the air and even the fire. What a job I had this morning, getting up, I had to make a big effort. It was really painful. I'd never have made up my mind if the sheets hadn't been damp too. I never imagined that, suddenly, as if by magic, I should find myself in the midst of spring, in the middle of April, the April of my dreams . . . my earliest dreams . . .

ARCHITECT: Dreams! [*Shrugging his shoulders.*] Anyhow, it would have been better if you'd come sooner, come before . . .

BÉRENGER: [*interrupting him*] Ah yes, I've lost a lot of time, that's true . . .

[BÉRENGER *and the* ARCHITECT *go on walking about the stage.* BÉRENGER *should give the impression he is walking through tree-lined avenues and parks. The* ARCHITECT *follows him, more slowly. At times* BÉRENGER *will have to turn round to speak to the* ARCHITECT *in a louder voice. He should appear to be waiting for the* ARCHITECT *to come closer. Pointing to empty space:*]

BÉRENGER: *There's* an attractive house! The façade is delightful, such a wonderfully pure style. Eighteenth century? No, fifteenth or the end of the nineteenth? It's classical anyway, and then it's so neat, so smart . . . Ah yes, I've lost a lot of time, is it too late? . . . No . . . Yes . . . No, it may not be too late, what do you think?

ARCHITECT: I haven't given the matter much thought.

BÉRENGER: I'm thirty-five years old, Monsieur, thirty-five . . . Actually to tell the truth, I'm forty, forty-five, perhaps a little more.

ARCHITECT: [*consulting the card*] We know. Your age is on the card. We have files on everyone.

BÉRENGER: Really? Oh!

ARCHITECT: It's quite usual, we have to have them for the record, but don't worry, the code provides no penalties for that kind of prevarication, not for vanity.

BÉRENGER: Thank goodness for that! Anyway, if I only admit to thirty-five, it's certainly not to deceive my fellow citizens, what's it matter to them? It's to deceive myself. In this way I act on myself by suggestion, I believe myself to be younger, I cheer myself up . . .

ARCHITECT: It's only human, only natural. [*The pocket telephone rings; the* ARCHITECT *takes it out again.*]

BÉRENGER: Oh, what nice little stones on the paths!

ARCHITECT: [*to telephone*] Hullo? . . . A woman? Take a

description of her. Enter it up. Send it to the statistics department . . .

BÉRENGER: [*pointing to the corner of the stage on the left*] What's that over there?

ARCHITECT: [*to telephone*] No, no, no, nothing else to report. All the time *I'm* here, nothing else *can* happen. [*He puts the receiver back in his pocket. To* BÉRENGER:] I'm sorry, I'm listening now.

BÉRENGER: [*as before*] What's that over there?

ARCHITECT: Oh, that . . . It's a greenhouse.

BÉRENGER: A greenhouse?

ARCHITECT: Yes. For the flowers that can't get used to a temperate climate, the flowers that like the cold. We've created a wintry climate for them. Now and again we have a little storm . . .

BÉRENGER: Ah, everything's been thought of . . . yes, Monsieur, I could be sixty years old, seventy, eighty, a hundred and twenty, how do I know?

ARCHITECT: Morally speaking!

BÉRENGER: It can be interpreted physically too. It's psychosomatic . . . Am I talking nonsense?

ARCHITECT: Not particularly. Like everyone else.

BÉRENGER: I feel old. Time is above all subjective. Or rather I *used* to feel old. Since this morning I'm a new man. I'm sure I'm becoming myself again. The world's becoming itself again; it's all thanks to *your* power. Your magic light . . .

ARCHITECT: My electric light!

BÉRENGER: . . . Your radiant city. [*He points quite near.*] It's the power of those immaculate walls covered with roses, your masterpiece! Ah, yes, yes, yes! . . . nothing's really lost, I'm sure of that now . . . Now, in fact, I *do* remember, two or three people did tell me about the smiling city;

some said it was quite near, others that it was far away,
that it was easy to get to, hard to find, that it was a district
specially reserved . . .

ARCHITECT: Not true!

BÉRENGER: . . . That there was no means of transport . . .

ARCHITECT: Nonsense. There's a tram stop over there, at
the end of the main thoroughfare.

BÉRENGER: Yes, of course, of course! I know *now*. For a long
time, I tell you, I tried consciously or unconsciously to
find the way. I would walk right to the end of a street, and
then realize it was a dead end. I'd follow a wall or a fence
until I reached the river far from the bridge, away beyond
the market and the gates of the town. Or else I'd meet
some friends on the way, who hadn't seen me since our
army days; I'd be forced to stop and chat to them until it
was too late and I had to go home. Still, what does it
matter now? I'm *here*. My worries are over.

ARCHITECT: It was really so simple. You only had to drop
me a line, write an official letter to the municipal offices,
and one of my departments would have sent you all the
necessary information by registered post.

BÉRENGER: Why yes, I only needed to think of that! Oh
well, no good crying over lost years . . .

ARCHITECT: How did you set about finding the way today?

BÉRENGER: Pure accident. I just took the tram.

ARCHITECT: What did I tell you?

BÉRENGER: Took the wrong tram, I meant to take another,
I was sure it wasn't going the right way, and yet it *was*, by
mistake, a lucky mistake . . .

ARCHITECT: Lucky?

BÉRENGER: No? Not lucky? But it *was*. Very, very lucky.

ARCHITECT: Oh well, you'll see for yourself, later.

BÉRENGER: I've seen already. I'm firmly convinced.

ARCHITECT: Anyway, remember you must always go as far as the terminus. Whatever the circumstances. All trams lead this way: it's the depot.

BÉRENGER: I know. The tram brought me here, to this stop. Although I hadn't been here before, I recognized everything at once; the avenues and the houses all blossoming, and you, looking as if you expected me.

ARCHITECT: I'd been informed.

BÉRENGER: It's such a transformation! It's as though I was far away in the South, two or three thousand miles away. Another universe, a world transfigured! And just that very short journey to get here, a journey that isn't *really*, since you might say it takes place in the same place . . . [*He laughs; then embarrassed:*] Forgive me, that wasn't very funny.

ARCHITECT: Don't look so upset. I've heard worse. I'll put it down to your state of bliss . . .

BÉRENGER: I've no mind for science. I suppose that's why in spite of your very pertinent explanations, *I* can't explain how the weather can always be fine here! Perhaps—this may have made it easier for you—perhaps it's a more sheltered spot? And yet it's not surrounded by hills to protect it from bad weather! Besides, hills don't chase the clouds away or stop it raining, everyone knows that. Is it that there are bright warm waves of air coming from a fifth point of the compass or some third stratum of the upper air? No, I suppose there aren't. Everyone would know about it. I'm really stupid. There's no breeze, although the air smells good. I must say it's odd, Monsieur, it's very odd!

ARCHITECT: [*giving the authoritative information*] I tell you there's nothing unusual about it, it's a technical matter! So try and understand. You ought to have taken an Adult

74

Education Course. It's just that this is a little island . . .
with concealed ventilators I copied from the ones in those
oases that crop up all over the place in the desert, where
suddenly out of the dry sand you see amazing cities rising
up, smothered with dewy roses, girdled with springs and
rivers and lakes . . .

BÉRENGER: Oh yes . . . That's true. You mean those cities
that are also called mirages. I've read explorers' tales
about them. You see, I'm not completely uneducated.
Mirages . . . there's nothing more real than a mirage.
Flowers on fire, trees in flame, pools of light, that's all
there really is that matters. I'm sure of it. And over there?
What's that?

ARCHITECT: Over where? Where? Oh, over there?

BÉRENGER: Looks like an ornamented pool.

[*By means of the lighting, the vague outline of an ornamental
pool appears at the back of the stage just as he says these words.*]

ARCHITECT: Er . . . yes, it *is* a pool. You recognized it. It's a
pool, all right. [*He consults his watch.*] I think I still have a
few minutes.

BÉRENGER: Can we go and see?

ARCHITECT: You want to have a closer look? [*He appears to
hesitate.*] Very well. If you insist, I'll have to show it you.

BÉRENGER: Or instead . . . I don't know what to choose . . .
It's all so beautiful . . . I like ornamental pools, but I
rather like the look of that flowering hawthorn too. If
you don't mind, we can look at the pool later . . .

ARCHITECT: As you like.

BÉRENGER: I love hawthorn bushes.

ARCHITECT: You've only to make up your mind.

BÉRENGER: Yes, yes, let's go over to the hawthorn.

ARCHITECT: I'm completely at your service.

BÉRENGER: One can't see everything at once.

ARCHITECT: True enough.

[*The pool disappears. They walk a few steps.*]

BÉRENGER: What a sweet smell! You know, Monsieur, I . . . forgive me for talking about myself . . . one can say anything to an architect, he understands everything.

ARCHITECT: Do please carry on. Don't be shy.

BÉRENGER: Thank you! You know, I do so need another life, a new life. Different surroundings, a different setting. A different setting, you'll think that's not much to ask, and that . . . with money, for example . . .

ARCHITECT: No, not at all . . .

BÉRENGER: Yes, yes, you're too polite . . . A setting, *that's* just superficial, an artistic consideration, unless it's, how shall I say, a setting, a background that would answer some profound need inside, which would be somehow . . .

ARCHITECT: I see, I see . . .

BÉRENGER: . . . the projection, the continuation of the universe inside you. Only, to project this universe within, some outside help is needed: some kind of material, physical light, a world that is objectively new. Gardens, blue sky, or the spring, which corresponds to the universe inside and offers a chance of recognition, which is like a translation or an anticipation of that universe, or a mirror in which its own smile could be reflected . . . in which it can find itself again and say: that's what I am in reality and I'd forgotten, a smiling being in a smiling world . . . Come to think of it, it's quite wrong to talk of a world within and a world without, separate worlds; there's an initial impulse, of course, which starts from us, and when it can't project itself, when it can't fulfil itself objectively, when there's not total agreement between myself inside and myself outside, then it's a catastrophe, a universal contradiction, a schism.

76

ARCHITECT: [*scratching his head*] What a vocabulary you have. We don't talk the same language.

BÉRENGER: I felt I couldn't go on living, and yet I couldn't die. Luckily it's all going to be different now.

ARCHITECT: Don't get too excited!

BÉRENGER: I'm sorry. I get carried away.

ARCHITECT: That's characteristic of you. You're one of those poetic personalities. As they exist, I suppose they must be necessary.

BÉRENGER: Year after year of dirty snow and bitter winds, of a climate indifferent to human beings . . . streets and houses and whole districts of people who aren't really unhappy, but worse, who are neither happy nor unhappy, people who are ugly because they're neither ugly nor beautiful, creatures that are dismally neutral, who long without longings as though they're unconscious, unconsciously suffering from being alive. But *I* was aware of the sickness of life. Perhaps because I'm more intelligent, or just the opposite, *less* intelligent, not so wise, not so resigned, not so patient. Is that a fault or a virtue?

ARCHITECT: [*giving signs of impatience*] Depends.

BÉRENGER: You can't tell. The winter of the soul! I'm not expressing myself clearly, am I?

ARCHITECT: I'm not capable of judging. It's not one of my duties. The logic department sees to that.

BÉRENGER: Perhaps you don't appreciate my lyrical side?

ARCHITECT: [*dryly*] Why yes, of course!

BÉRENGER: Well, you see: once upon a time there was a blazing fire inside me. The cold could do nothing against it, a youthfulness, a spring no autumn could touch; a source of light, glowing wells of joy that seemed inexhaustible. Not happiness, I mean joy, felicity, which made it possible for me to live . . .

[*The telephone rings in the* ARCHITECT'*s pocket.*]

There was enormous energy there . . .

[*The* ARCHITECT *takes the telephone from his pocket.*]

A force . . . it must have been the life force, mustn't it?

ARCHITECT: [*holding the receiver to his ear*] Hullo?

BÉRENGER: And then it grew weaker and all died away.

ARCHITECT: [*to the telephone*] Hullo? Fine, fine, fine! . . .
Don't tell me that only happened yesterday!

BÉRENGER: [*continuing his monologue*] Oh it must go back
. . . I don't know how long . . . a long, long time
ago . . .

[*The* ARCHITECT *puts the receiver back in his pocket and
shows fresh signs of impatience; he goes into the wings on the
left and brings on a chair, which he sets down in the left-hand
corner, where the greenhouse was supposed to be.*]

Must be centuries ago . . . or perhaps only a few years,
perhaps it was yesterday . . .

ARCHITECT: I must ask you to excuse me, I'm afraid I must
go to my office. I've some urgent matters to attend to. [*He
goes off left for a moment.*]

BÉRENGER: [*alone*] Oh . . . Monsieur, really, I'm so sorry,
I . . .

ARCHITECT: [*coming back with a small table, which he sets in front
of the chair; he sits down, takes the telephone from his pocket,
puts it on the table and lays his briefcase open before him*] It's for
me to apologize.

BÉRENGER: Oh, no! I feel terrible about it!

ARCHITECT: Don't let it upset you too much. I have two
ears; one for duty, and the other I reserve for you. One
eye too, for you. The other's for the borough.

BÉRENGER: It won't tire you too much?

ARCHITECT: Don't worry. I'm used to it. All right, carry on
. . . [*He takes from his briefcase, or pretends to, some files which*

he lays out on the table and opens.) I'm attending to my files, and to you too . . . You were saying you didn't know how long ago it was this force died away!

BÉRENGER: It certainly wasn't yesterday. [*He goes on walking, from now on, round and round the* ARCHITECT, *who is plunged in his files.*] It's such an old story, I've almost forgotten, it might have been an illusion; and yet it can't be an illusion when I still feel the loss of it so badly.

ARCHITECT: [*in his files*] Go on.

BÉRENGER: I can't analyse the feeling, I don't even know if the experience I had can be communicated. It wasn't very frequent. It happened, five or six, ten times perhaps in my life. Often enough, though, to fill to overflowing Heaven knows what secret reservoirs of my mind with joy and conviction. When I was in a gloomy mood, the memory of that dazzling radiance, that glowing feeling, gave fresh life to the force within me, to those reasonless reasons for living and loving . . . loving what? . . . Loving everything wholeheartedly . . .

ARCHITECT: [*to the telephone*] Hullo, the supplies have run out!

BÉRENGER: Yes, I'm afraid they have, Monsieur.

ARCHITECT: [*who has hung up*] I wasn't saying that to you, it's about my files.

BÉRENGER: It's true for me too, Monsieur, the reservoirs are empty. I'm not economically sound any more. My supplies of light have run out. I'll try and explain . . . I'm not imposing on you?

ARCHITECT: It's going in the record. That's my job. Carry on, don't mind me.

BÉRENGER: It happened as spring was ending, or perhaps in the very first days of summer, just before midday; it all came about in a way that was perfectly simple and perfectly unexpected as well. The sky was as pure as the one you've managed to cover your radiant city with, Monsieur. Yes, it happened in extra-ordinary silence, in a long, long second of silence . . .

ARCHITECT: [*still in his files*] Right. Fine.

BÉRENGER: The last time I must have been seventeen or eighteen, and I was in a little country town . . . which one? . . . I wonder which it was? . . . Somewhere in the South, I think . . . It's of no importance anyway, the place hardly counts. I was walking along a narrow street, which was both old and new, with low houses on either side, all white and tucked away in courtyards or little gardens, with wooden fences, painted . . . pale yellow, was it pale yellow? I was all alone in the street. I was walking along by the fences and the houses, and it was fine, not too hot, with the sun above, high above my head in the blue of the sky. I was walking fast, but where was I going? I don't remember. I was deeply aware of the unique joy of being alive. I'd forgotten everything, all I could think of was those houses, that deep sky and that sun, which seemed to be coming nearer, within my grasp, in a world that was made for me.

ARCHITECT: [*consulting his watch*] She's not here yet! Late again!

BÉRENGER: [*continuing*] Suddenly the joy became more intense, breaking all bounds! And then, oh what indescribable bliss took hold of me! The light grew more and more brilliant, and still lost none of its softness, it was so dense you could almost breathe it, it had become the air itself, you could drink it like clear water . . . How can I convey its incomparable brilliance? . . . It's as if there were four suns in the sky . . .

ARCHITECT: [*speaking into the telephone*] Hullo? Have you

seen my secretary today? There's a pile of work waiting. [*He hangs up angrily.*]

BÉRENGER: The houses I was passing were like immaterial shades ready to melt away in that mightier light which governed all.

ARCHITECT: I'll make her pay a nice fat fine!

BÉRENGER: [*to* ARCHITECT] You see what I mean?

ARCHITECT: [*vaguely*] More or less. Your story seems clearer now.

BÉRENGER: Not a man in the street, not a cat, not a sound, there was only me.

[*The telephone bell rings.*]

And yet I didn't suffer from being alone, I didn't feel lonely.

ARCHITECT: [*to the telephone*] Well, has she arrived?

BÉRENGER: My own peace and light spread in their turn throughout the world, I was filling the universe with a kind of ethereal energy. Not an empty corner,everything was a mingling of airiness and plenitude, perfectly balanced.

ARCHITECT: [*to the telephone*] At last! Put her on the line.

BÉRENGER: A song of triumph rose from the depths of my being: I *was*, I realized I had always *been*, that I was no longer going to die.

ARCHITECT: [*on the telephone, mastering his irritation*] I must say I'm very pleased to hear your voice, Mademoiselle. It's about time. What?

BÉRENGER: Everything was virgin, purified, discovered anew. I had a feeling of inexpressible surprise, yet at the same time it was all quite familiar to me.

ARCHITECT: [*on the telephone*] What do you mean by that, Mademoiselle?

BÉRENGER: That's *it* all right, I said to myself, that's *it*, all right . . . I can't tell *you* what I mean by 'it', but I promise you, Monsieur *I* understood quite well what I meant.

ARCHITECT: [*on the telephone*] I don't understand you, Mademoiselle. You've no reason to be dissatisfied with us, I should say the boot's on the other foot.

BÉRENGER: I felt I was there at the gates, at the very centre of the universe . . . That must seem contradictory to you?

ARCHITECT: [*on the telephone*] One moment, please. [*To* BÉRENGER:] I follow you, I follow you, don't worry, I get the general idea. [*On the telephone:*] Hullo, yes?

BÉRENGER: I walked and ran and cried: I *am*, I *am*, *everything* is, everything *is*! . . . Oh, I'm sure I could have flown away, I'd lost so much weight, I was lighter than the blue sky I was breathing . . . The slightest effort, the tiniest little leap would have been enough . . . I should have taken off . . . I'm sure I should.

ARCHITECT: [*on the telephone, banging his fist on the table*] Now that's going too far! What's made you feel like this?

BÉRENGER: If I didn't do it, it's because I was too happy, it didn't even enter my head.

ARCHITECT: [*on the telephone*] You want to leave the Service? Think carefully before you resign. Without any good reason you're abandoning a brilliant career! After all, with us your future is insured, *and* your life . . . your life! You aren't afraid of the danger!

BÉRENGER: And suddenly, or rather gradually . . . no, it was all at once, I don't know, I only know that everything went grey and pale and neutral again. Not really, of course, the sky was still pure, but it wasn't the same purity, it wasn't the same sun, the same morning, the same spring. It was like a conjuring trick. The light was the same as on any other day, ordinary daylight.

ARCHITECT: [*on the telephone*] You can't stand the situation any longer? That's childish. I refuse your resignation. Come and clear up the day's mail anyway, and you can explain yourself. I'm waiting for you. [*He hangs up.*]

BÉRENGER: There was a kind of chaotic vacuum inside me, I was overcome with the immense sadness you feel at a moment of tragic and intolerable separation. The old gossips came out of their courtyards and split my eardrums with their screeching voices, the dogs barked, and I felt lost among all those people, all those *things* . . .

ARCHITECT: She's a stupid girl. [*He stands up.*] Still, it's her own affair. There are thousands more after her job . . . [*He sits down again.*] . . . and a life without peril.

BÉRENGER: And since then, it's been perpetual November, perpetual twilight, twilight in the morning, twilight at midnight, at noon. The light of dawn has gone! And to think we call this civilization!

ARCHITECT: We're still waiting!

BÉRENGER: It's only the memory of what happened that's helped me to go on living in this grey city.

ARCHITECT: [*to* BÉRENGER] You got over it, just the same, this . . . melancholy?

BÉRENGER: Not entirely. But I promised myself I wouldn't forget. I told myself that on the days I felt sad and nervous, depressed and anxious, I would always remember that glorious moment. It would help me to bear everything, give me a reason for living, and be a comfort to me. For years I felt sure . . .

ARCHITECT: Sure of what?

BÉRENGER: Sure I'd been sure . . . but the memory wasn't strong enough to stand the test of time.

ARCHITECT: But it seems to me . . .

BÉRENGER: You're wrong, Monsieur. The memory I've kept is nothing now but the memory of a memory, like a thought grown foreign to me, like a tale told by another, a faded picture whose brightness I could no longer restore. The water in the well had dried up and I was dying of thirst . . . But *you* must understand me perfectly, this light is in *you* too, it's the same as mine, because [*a broad gesture taking in empty space*] you have obviously re-created and materialized it. This radiant district must have sprung from you . . . You've given me back that forgotten light . . . almost. I'm terribly grateful to you. In my name and in the name of all who live here, I thank you.

ARCHITECT: Why yes, of course.

BÉRENGER: And with you, it's not the unreal product of an overheated imagination. These are real houses and stones and bricks and cement. [*Touching empty space.*] It's concrete, solid, tangible. Yours is the right system, your methods are rational. [*He still appears to be feeling the walls.*]

ARCHITECT: [*also feeling the invisible walls, after leaving his corner*] It's brick, yes, and good brick too. Cement, the best quality.

BÉRENGER: [*as before*] No, no, it's not just a dream, this time.

ARCHITECT: [*still feeling the invisible walls, then stopping with a sigh*] Perhaps it would have been better if it had been a dream. It's all the same to me. I'm a civil servant. But for a lot of other people, reality, unlike dreams, can turn into a nightmare . . .

BÉRENGER: [*who also stops feeling the invisible walls, greatly surprised*] Why, what do you mean?

[*The* ARCHITECT *returns to his files.*]

In any case, I'm glad my memory is real and I can feel it with my fingers. I'm as young as I was a hundred years ago. I can fall in love again . . . [*Calling to the wings on the right:*] Mademoiselle, oh, Mademoiselle, will you marry me?

[*Just as he finishes this last sentence,* DANY *comes in from the right. She is the* ARCHITECT's *blonde secretary.*]

ARCHITECT: [*to* DANY *as she enters*] Oh, so there you are! I've got something to say to you!

DANY: [*to* BÉRENGER] Do give me time to think it over!

ARCHITECT: [*to* BÉRENGER] My secretary, Mademoiselle Dany. [*To* DANY]: Monsieur Bérenger.

DANY: [*absentmindedly, rather nervously, to* BÉRENGER] Pleased to meet you.

ARCHITECT: [*to* DANY] In the Civil Service we don't like people to be late, Mademoiselle, or impulsive either.

BÉRENGER: [*to* DANY, *who goes and sets her typewriter on the table, and fetches a chair from the wings on the left*] Mademoiselle Dany, what a lovely name! Have you thought it over yet? The answer's 'Yes' isn't it?

DANY: [*to the* ARCHITECT] I've made up my mind to leave, Monsieur, I need a holiday, I'm tired.

ARCHITECT: [*sweetly*] If that's all it is, you should have told me. We can arrange something. Would you like three days off?

BÉRENGER: [*to* DANY] It is Yes, isn't it? Oh, you're so beautiful.

DANY: [*to* ARCHITECT] I must have a much longer rest than that.

ARCHITECT: [*to* DANY] I'll apply to the Departmental Board, I can get you a week—half-pay.

DANY: [*to* ARCHITECT] I need a permanent rest.

BÉRENGER: [*to* DANY] I like fair girls, with glowing faces, bright eyes and long legs!

ARCHITECT: Permanent? I see! . . .

DANY: [*to* ARCHITECT] I simply must do some different work. I can't stand the situation any longer.

ARCHITECT: Oh, so that's it.

DANY: [*to* ARCHITECT] Yes, Monsieur.

BÉRENGER: [*to* DANY, *enthusiastically*] You said Yes! Oh, Mademoiselle Dany . . .

ARCHITECT: [*to* BÉRENGER] She's talking to me, not to you.

DANY: [*to* ARCHITECT] I always hoped things might change, but they're still the same. I don't see any chance of improvement.

ARCHITECT: Now think, I'm telling you again, think carefully! If you no longer belong to our organization, the Civil Service can no longer take you under its wing. Do you realize? Are you fully aware of the dangers that lie in wait?

DANY: Yes, Monsieur, no one's in a better position than I am to know about that.

ARCHITECT: You're willing to take the risk?

DANY: [*to* ARCHITECT] I am, yes, Monsieur.

BÉRENGER: [*to* DANY] Say Yes to me too. You say it so nicely.

ARCHITECT: [*to* DANY] Then I refuse all responsibility. You have been warned.

DANY: [*to* ARCHITECT] I'm not deaf, I understand, you needn't repeat yourself!

BÉRENGER: [*to* ARCHITECT] Isn't she sweet! Delightful. [*To* DANY:] Mademoiselle, Mademoiselle, we'll live here, in this district, in this villa! We'll be happy at last.

ARCHITECT: [*to* DANY] So you really won't change your mind? It's a crazy, headstrong thing to do!

DANY: [*to* ARCHITECT] No, Monsieur.

BÉRENGER: [*to* DANY] Oh, you didn't say No?

ARCHITECT: [*to* BÉRENGER] She said No to *me*.

BÉRENGER: Ah, that's all right, then!

DANY: [*to* ARCHITECT] I hate the Civil Service, I detest your beautiful district, I can't stand any more, I can't bear it!

ARCHITECT: [*to* DANY] It's not *my* district.

BÉRENGER: [*to* DANY, *who is not listening*] Give me your answer, beautiful Demoiselle, Dany the magnificent, Dany the sublime . . . May I call you Dany?

ARCHITECT: [*to* DANY] I can't stop you resigning, so you'd better go, but keep a sharp look-out. That's a piece of friendly advice I'm giving you, fatherly advice.

BÉRENGER: [*to* ARCHITECT] Were you decorated for your achievements in urban development? You should have been.

DANY: [*to* ARCHITECT] If you like, I'll finish typing the letters before I go.

BÉRENGER: [*to* ARCHITECT] If I'd been the Mayor, I'd have decorated you all right.

ARCHITECT: [*to* BÉRENGER] Thank you. [*To* DANY:] You needn't bother, thank you. I'll manage.

BÉRENGER: [*smelling imaginary flowers*] What a lovely smell! Are they lilies?

ARCHITECT: No, violets.

DANY: [*to* ARCHITECT] I was only trying to be helpful.

BÉRENGER: [*to* ARCHITECT] May I pick some for Dany?

ARCHITECT: If you like.

BÉRENGER: [*to* DANY] You don't know, my dear, dear Dany, dear finacée, how I've longed for you.

DANY: If that's how you take it . . . [*In some irritation she briskly puts her things in order and picks up her typewriter.*]

BÉRENGER: [*to* DANY] We'll live in a wonderful flat, full of sunshine.

DANY: [*to* ARCHITECT] Surely you can understand I can't go on sharing the responsibility. It's too much for me.

ARCHITECT: The Civil Service is not responsible for that.

DANY: [*to* ARCHITECT] You ought to be able to realize . . .

ARCHITECT: [*to* DANY] It's not for you to give *me* advice. That's *my* business. But I warn you again; watch your step.

DANY: [*to* ARCHITECT] I'm not taking advice from you either. It's *my* business too.

ARCHITECT: [*to* DANY] All right, all right!

DANY: Au revoir, Monsieur.

ARCHITECT: Goodbye.

DANY: [*to* BÉRENGER] Au revoir, Monsieur.

BÉRENGER: [*running after* DANY, *who is making for the exit on the right*] Dany, Mademoiselle, don't go before you've given me an answer . . . At least, please take these violets.

[DANY *goes out.* BÉRENGER *stands near the exit, his arms hanging loosely.*]

Oh . . . [*To* ARCHITECT:] You understand the human heart; when a woman doesn't answer Yes or No, it means Yes, doesn't it? [*Calling towards the wings on the right:*] You'll be my inspiration, my Muse. I'll really *work.* [*While a slight echo is heard repeating the previous words,* BÉRENGER *moves two paces nearer the* ARCHITECT *and indicates the empty space:*] I'll not give up. I'm settling down here with Dany. I'll buy that white house, with the trees and grass all round, the one that looks abandoned by the builders . . . I haven't much money, you'll let me pay in instalments.

ARCHITECT: If you really want to! If you're not going to change your mind.

BÉRENGER: I'm determined. Why should I change my mind? With your permission, I want to be a citizen of the radiant

city. I'll move in tomorrow, even if the house isn't quite
ready yet.

ARCHITECT: [*looking at his watch*] Twenty-five to one.
[*Suddenly, there is the noise of a stone falling a few paces from*
BÉRENGER, *between him and the* ARCHITECT.]

BÉRENGER: Oh! [*Starts back a little.*] A stone!

ARCHITECT: [*impassively, without surprise*] Yes, a stone!

BÉRENGER: [*leans forward and picks up the stone, then straightens
up and inspects it in his hand*] It is a stone!

ARCHITECT: Haven't you seen one before?

BÉRENGER: Yes . . . of course . . . What? They're throwing
stones at us?

ARCHITECT: *A* stone, just one stone, not stones!

BÉRENGER: I understand, they threw a stone at us.

ARCHITECT: Don't worry. They're not really going to stone
you. It didn't touch you, did it?

BÉRENGER: It could have.

ARCHITECT: No, no, of course it couldn't. It *cannot* touch
you. It's only teasing.

BÉRENGER: Oh, I see! . . . If it's only teasing, then I suppose
I can take a joke! [*He drops the stone.*] I don't easily take
offence. Especially in these surroundings it takes a lot to
upset you. She will write to me, won't she? [*He casts a
rather anxious look about him.*] It's so restful here, and intended to be that way. Almost a little too restful, don't
you think? Why can't you see a single soul in the streets?
We really are the only people out! . . . Oh yes, of course,
it must be because it's lunchtime. Everyone's eating. But
why can't we hear any laughter at table, any clinking of
glasses? Not a sound, not a whisper, not a voice singing.
And all the windows are shut! [*He looks round the empty
stage, surprised.*] I didn't notice before. It would be under-
standable in a dream, but not when it's real.

89

ARCHITECT: I'd have thought it was obvious.

[*The sound of broken window-panes is heard.*]

BÉRENGER: What's happening now?

ARCHITECT: [*taking the telephone from his pocket again; to* BÉRENGER] That's easy. You don't know what it is? A window's been smashed. It must have been broken by a stone.

[*The noise of another window being smashed;* BÉRENGER *starts back more violently.*]

[*On the telephone:*] Two broken windows.

BÉRENGER: What's it all about? A joke, I suppose? Two jokes! [*Another stone knocks his hat off; he picks up the hat quickly and puts it back on his head.*] Three jokes!

ARCHITECT: [*putting the telephone back in his pocket and frowning*] Now listen, Monsieur. You and I are not business men. We're civil servants, bureaucrats. So I must tell you officially, bureaucratically, that the house that looked abandoned really has been abandoned by the builders. The police have suspended all construction work. I knew this before, but I've just had it confirmed by phone.

BÉRENGER: What? . . . Why?

ARCHITECT: It's an unnecessary step to take anyway. You're the only one wants to buy any property now. I don't suppose you know what it's all about . . .

BÉRENGER: What *is* it all about?

ARCHITECT: Actually, the people who live in this district want to leave it . . .

BÉRENGER: Leave the radiant district? The people want to leave it . . .

ARCHITECT: Yes. They've no other homes to go to. Otherwise they'd *all* have packed their bags. Perhaps too they may make it a point of honour not to run away. They'd rather stay and hide in their beautiful flats. They only

come out when they really have to, in groups of ten or
fifteen at a time. And even that doesn't make for safety. . .

BÉRENGER: What's so dangerous? Just another joke, isn't
it! Why are you looking so serious? You're clouding the
whole place over! You're trying to frighten me! . . .

ARCHITECT: [*solemnly*] A civil servant doesn't make jokes.

BÉRENGER: [*terribly upset*] What are you talking about?
You're really upsetting me! It's you who just threw that
stone at me . . . Morally speaking of course! Oh dear, and
I already felt I'd taken root in these surroundings! Now
all the brilliance they offer is dead, and they're nothing
more than an empty frame . . . I feel shut out!

ARCHITECT: I'm very sorry. Steady there!

BÉRENGER: I've a horrible premonition.

ARCHITECT: I'm so sorry, so sorry.

[*During the previous dialogue and what comes after, the acting
should never lose a touch of irony, which should especially
balance the pathetic moments.*]

BÉRENGER: I can feel the darkness spreading inside me again!

ARCHITECT: [*dryly*] Sorry, very sorry, so sorry.

BÉRENGER: Please, you must explain. I was so hoping to
spend a nice day! . . . I was so happy a few moments ago.

ARCHITECT: [*pointing*] You see this ornamental pool?

[*The pool reappears, clearly this time.*]

BÉRENGER: It's the same one we went past already, just now!

ARCHITECT: I wanted to show you then . . . You preferred
the hawthorns . . . [*He points to the pool again:*] It's there in
the pool every day, that two or three people are found,
drowned.

BÉRENGER: Drowned?

ARCHITECT: Come and look if you don't believe me. Come
on, come closer!

BÉRENGER: [*accompanying the* ARCHITECT *to the place indicated or right to the front of the stage, while the objects referred to appear as they are mentioned*] Go nearer!

ARCHITECT: Look! What do you see?

BÉRENGER: Oh, Heavens!

ARCHITECT: Come on now, no fainting, be a man!

BÉRENGER: [*with an effort*] I can see . . . it's not true . . . Yes, I can see, on the water, the dead body of a little boy, floating in his hoop . . . a little chap of five or six . . . He's clutching the stick in his hand . . . Next to him the bloated corpse of an officer in the engineers in full uniform . . .

ARCHITECT: There are even three today. [*Pointing.*] Over there!

BÉRENGER: It's a plant in the water!

ARCHITECT: Look again.

BÉRENGER: Good God! . . . Yes . . . I see! It's red hair streaming up from the bottom, stuck to the marble edge of the pool. How horrible! It must be a woman.

ARCHITECT: [*shrugging his shoulders*] Obviously. And one's a man. And the other's a child. *We* don't know any more than that, either.

BÉRENGER: Perhaps it's the boy's mother! Poor devils! Why didn't you tell me before?

ARCHITECT: But I told you! You were always stopping me, always admiring the beautiful surroundings.

BÉRENGER: Poor devils! [*Violently.*] Who did it?

ARCHITECT: The murderer, the thug. Always the same elusive character.

BÉRENGER: But our lives are in danger! Let's go! [*He takes to his heels, runs a few yards across the stage and comes back to the* ARCHITECT, *who has not moved.*] Let's go! [*He takes flight again, but runs round and round the* ARCHITECT, *who takes out a cigarette and lights it. A shot is heard.*] He's shooting!

ARCHITECT: Don't be afraid. You're in no danger while you're with me.

BÉRENGER: What about that shot? Oh, no . . . no . . . You don't make me feel safer! [*He moves restlessly about and starts shaking.*]

ARCHITECT: It's only a game . . . Yes . . . Just now, it's only a game, to tease you! I'm the City Architect, a municipal civil servant, he doesn't attack the Civil Service. When I've retired, it'll be different, but for the moment . . .

BÉRENGER; Let's go. Get away from here. I can't wait to leave your beautiful district . . .

ARCHITECT: There you are, you see, you *have* changed your mind!

BÉRENGER: You mustn't hold it against me!

ARCHITECT: I don't care. I haven't been asked to detail volunteers and compel them to live here by choice. No one's obliged to live dangerously if he doesn't want that sort of life! . . . When the district's completely depopulated, they'll pull it down.

BÉRENGER: [*still hurrying round and round the* ARCHITECT] Depopulated?

ARCHITECT: People will decide to leave it in the end . . . or they'll all be killed. Oh, it'll take a bit of time . . .

BÉRENGER: Let's be off, quick! [*He goes round and round, faster and faster, with his head well down.*] The rich aren't always happy either, nor are the people who live in the residential districts . . . or the radiant ones . . . There are no radiant ones! . . . It's even worse than the other districts, in ours, the busy crowded ones! . . . Oh, Monsieur, I feel so upset about it. I feel shattered, stunned . . . My tiredness has come on again . . . There's no point in living! What's the good of it all, what's the good if it's only to bring us to this? Stop it, you must stop it, Superintendent.

ARCHITECT: Easy to say.

BÉRENGER: I suppose you *are* the police superintendent of the district too?

ARCHITECT: As a matter of fact, that is also one of my duties. It always is for special architects like me.

BÉRENGER: You're really hoping to arrest him before you retire?

ARCHITECT: [*coldly annoyed*] Naturally, we're doing all we can! . . . Look out, not that way, you'll get lost, you're always going round in circles, going back in your own tracks.

BÉRENGER: [*pointing quite close to him*] Ooh! Is that still the same pool?

ARCHITECT: One's enough for him.

BÉRENGER: Are those the same bodies as just now?

ARCHITECT: Three a day is a fair average, what more do you want?

BÉRENGER: Show me the way! . . . Let's go! . . .

ARCHITECT: [*taking him by the arm and guiding him*] This way.

BÉRENGER: And the day started so well! I shall always see those people drowned, I shall always have that picture in my mind.

ARCHITECT: That's what comes of being so emotional!

BÉRENGER: Never mind, it's better to know it all, better to know it all! . . .

[*The lighting changes. Now it is grey, and there are faint sounds of the street and the trams.*]

ARCHITECT: Here we are! We're not in the radiant city any more, we've gone through the gates. [*He lets go of* BÉRENGER'*s arm.*] We're on the outer boulevard. You see, over there? There's your tram. That's the stop.

BÉRENGER: Where?

ARCHITECT: There, where those people are waiting. It's the

terminus. The tram starts off in the opposite direction and takes you straight to the other end of town, takes you home!

[*You can just see, in perspective, some streets beneath a rainy sky, a few outlines and vague red lights. The designer should see that* very gradually *everything becomes more real. The change should be brought about by the lighting and with a very small number of props; shop-signs, and advertisements should slowly appear one after the other, but not more three or four in all.*]

BÉRENGER: I'm frozen.

ARCHITECT: You *are*. You're shivering.

BÉRENGER: It's the shock.

ARCHITECT: It's the cold, too. [*He stretches out his hand to feel the raindrops.*] It's raining, Half sleet, half snow.

[BÉRENGER *nearly slips over.*]

Be careful, it's slippery, the pavement's wet. [*He holds him up.*]

BÉRENGER: Thank you.

ARCHITECT: Put your overcoat on or you'll catch cold.

BÉRENGER: Thank you. [*He puts his overcoat on and feverishly ties his scarf round his neck.*] Brr. Goodbye, Monsieur Superintendent!

ARCHITECT: You're not going straight back home! No one's expecting you . . . You've plenty of time to have a drink. Do you good. Go on, let yourself go, it's time for that drink before dinner. There's a bistro over there, near the tram-stop, just by the cemetery. They sell wreaths too.

BÉRENGER: You seem to be in a good mood again. I'm not.

ARCHITECT: I was never in a bad one.

BÉRENGER: In spite of . . .

ARCHITECT: [*interrupting him, as the sign of the bistro lights up*] Have to look life in the face, you know! [*He lays his hand*

on the handle of an imaginary door, beneath the sign of the bistro.]
Let's go in.

BÉRENGER: I don't feel much like it . . .

ARCHITECT: Go on in.

BÉRENGER: After you, Monsieur Superintendent.

ARCHITECT: No please, after you.

[*He pushes him. Noise of the bistro door. They come into the shop: this may be the same corner of the stage where the imaginary greenhouse and then the* ARCHITECT'*s imaginary office was before. They go and sit down on two chairs by the little table. They are doubtless next to the big windows of the shop. In the event of the table and chairs having been removed previously, a folding table can be brought on by the* OWNER OF THE BISTRO *when he appears. Two folding chairs could also be picked up from the floor of the stage by* BÉRENGER *and the* ARCHITECT.]

Sit down, sit down. [*They sit down.*] You *do* look cheerful! Don't take it to heart so! If we thought about all the misfortunes of mankind we could never go on living. And we must live! All the time there are children with their throats cut, old men starving, mournful windows, orphan girls, people dying, justice miscarrying, houses collapsing on the tenants . . . mountains crumbling away . . . massacres, and floods, and dogs run over . . . That's how journalists earn their daily bread. Everything has it's bright side. In the end it's the bright side you've got to bear in mind.

BÉRENGER: Yes. Monsieur Superintendent, yes . . . but having been so close and seen with my own eyes . . . I can't remain indifferent. *You* may have got used to it, you with your two professions.

ARCHITECT: [*slapping* BÉRENGER *on the shoulder*] You're too impressionable, I've told you before. Got to face facts.

Come on now, pull yourself together, where's your will-power! [*He slaps him on the shoulder again.* BÉRENGER *nearly falls off the chair.*] You seem fit enough, whatever you say, although you look so sorry for yourself. You're healthy in mind and body!

BÉRENGER: I don't say I'm not. What I'm suffering from doesn't show, it's theoretical, spiritual.

ARCHITECT: I see.

BÉRENGER: You're being sarcastic.

ARCHITECT: I wouldn't dream of it. I've seen quite a few cases like yours among my patients.

BÉRENGER: Yes, of course, you're a doctor too.

ARCHITECT: When I've a minute to spare, I do a little general medicine, I took over from a psycho-analyst and was assistant to a surgeon in my youth, I've also studied sociology . . . Come on now, let's try and cheer you up. [*Clapping his hands.*] Monsieur!

BÉRENGER: I'm not as versatile as you.

[*From the wings on the left can be heard the voice of a* CLOCHARD.]

CLOCHARD: [*off*] When I left the Merchant Navy
I got spliced to young Octavie!

VOICE OF OWNER: [*loud voice*] Be right with you, Monsieur Superintendent! [*Change of tone; still in the wings to the* CLOCHARD:]

Get out of here, go and get drunk somewhere else!

CLOCHARD: [*off. Thick voice*] What's the point? I'm drunk already!

[*The drunken* CLOCHARD *appears from the left, brutally pushed on stage by the* OWNER, *a dark fat character with great hairy arms.*]

I got drunk at your place, paid for it, shouldn't have given me the stuff!

OWNER: I told you to get out! [*To* ARCHITECT:] Glad to see you, Monsieur Superintendent.

ARCHITECT: [*to* BÉRENGER] You see . . . We aren't in the beautiful district any more, people's manners aren't so good to start with.

CLOCHARD: [*still being pushed by the* OWNER] What you up to?

BÉRENGER: [*to* ARCHITECT] So I see!

OWNER: [*to* CLOCHARD] Off you go . . . Look, the Superintendent's over there!

CLOCHARD: Not doing anyone any harm! [*While still being pushed he stumbles and falls full length, but picks himself up without protest.*]

ARCHITECT: [*to* OWNER] Two Beaujolais.

OWNER: Right, sir. I've got some of the real stuff for you. [*To the* CLOCHARD, *who is getting up:*] Get out and close the door behind you, don't let me catch you again. [*He goes off left.*]

ARCHITECT: [*to* BÉRENGER] Still feeling depressed?

BÉRENGER: [*with a helpless gesture to the empty air*] What do you expect!

[*The* OWNER *appears with two glasses of wine, while the* CLOCHARD *closes the door in mime and leaves the shop.*]

OWNER: Your Beaujolais, Monsieur Superintendent!

CLOCHARD: [*going off right, still staggering and singing*]:

> When I left the Merchant Navy
> I got spliced to young Octavie!

OWNER: [*to* ARCHITECT] You want a snack, Monsieur Superintendent?

ARCHITECT: Give us a couple of sandwiches.

OWNER: I've got a first-class rabbit pâté, pure pork!

[BÉRENGER *shows signs of wanting to pay.*]

ARCHITECT: [*laying his hand on* BÉRENGER's *arm, to stop him*]

No, no, not you! This is on me! [*To* OWNER:] This is on me!

OWNER: Right, Monsieur Superintendent! [*He goes off left. The* ARCHITECT *takes a sip of the wine.* BÉRENGER *does not touch his.*]

BÉRENGER: [*after a short pause*] If only you had a description of him.

ARCHITECT: But we have. At least we know how he looks to his victims. Pictures of him have been stuck on all the walls. We've done our best.

BÉRENGER: How did you get them?

ARCHITECT: They were found on the bodies of the drowned. Some of the people have been brought back to life for a moment and they even provided other information. We know how he sets about it too. So does everyone in the district.

BÉRENGER: But why aren't they more careful? They only have to avoid him.

ARCHITECT: It's not so simple. I tell you, every evening there are always two or three who fall into the trap. But *he* never gets caught.

BÉRENGER: It's beyond me.

[*The* ARCHITECT *takes another sip of wine. The* PATRON *brings the two sandwiches and goes out.*]

I'm amazed . . . but you, Monsieur Superintendent, seem almost amused by the whole business.

ARCHITECT: I can't help it. After all, it is quite interesting. You see, it's there . . . Look through the window. [*He pretends to be pulling an imaginary curtain aside; or perhaps a real curtain could have appeared; he points to the left:*] You see it's there, at the tram-stop, he strikes. When the people get off to go home, they walk to the gates, because they're not allowed to use their private cars outside the radiant city, and that's when he comes to meet them, disguised as a beggar. He starts whining, as they all do, asks for alms and tries to rouse their pity. The usual thing: just out of hospital, no work, looking for a job, nowhere to spend the night. That's not what does the trick, that's only a start. He's feeling his way, he chooses a likely prey, gets into conversation, hangs on and won't be shaken off. He offers to sell a few small articles he takes from his basket, artificial flowers, birds, old-style nightcaps, maps . . . postcards . . . American cigarettes, obscene little drawings, all sorts of objects. Generally his offerings are refused, his client hurries on, no time to spare. Still haggling, they both arrive at the pool you already know. Then, suddenly, the big moment arrives; he suggests showing the Colonel's photo. This is irresistible. As it's getting rather dark, the client leans forward to get a better view. But now it's too late. A close scrutiny of the picture is a disturbing experience. Taking advantage of this he gives a push and the victim falls in the pool and is drowned. The blow is struck, all he has to do now is to look for fresh prey.

BÉRENGER: What's so extraordinary is that people know and still let themselves be taken in.

ARCHITECT: That's the trick, you know. He's never been caught in the act.

BÉRENGER: Incredible! Incredible!

ARCHITECT: And yet it's true! [*He bites into his sandwich.*] You're not drinking? Or eating?

[*Noise of a tram arriving at the stop.* BÉRENGER *instinctively raises his head quickly and goes to pull the curtain aside to look through the window in the direction of the tram-stop.*]

That's the tram arriving.

BÉRENGER: Groups of people are getting out!

ARCHITECT: Of course. The people who live in the district. Going home.

BÉRENGER: I can't see any beggars.

ARCHITECT: You won't. He'll not show himself. He knows we're here.

BÉRENGER: [*turning his back to the window and coming back to the* ARCHITECT, *who also has his back to the window, to sit down again*] Perhaps it would be a good idea if you had a plain-clothes inspector permanently on duty at this spot.

ARCHITECT: You want to teach me how to do my job? Technically, it's not possible. Our inspectors are over-worked, they've got other things to do. Besides, *they'd* want to see the Colonel's photo too. There have been five of them drowned already like that. Ah . . . If we could prove his identity, we'd know where to find him!

[*Suddenly a cry is heard, and the heavy sound of a body falling into water.*]

BÉRENGER: [*jumping to his feet*] Did you hear that?

ARCHITECT: [*still seated, biting his sandwich*] He's struck again. You see how easy it is to stop him. As soon as your back's turned, a second's inattention, and there you are . . . One second, that's all he needs.

BÉRENGER: It's terrible, terrible!

[*Muttering voices are heard, alarmed voices coming from the wings, the sound of footsteps, and a police car's screaming brakes.*]

[*Wringing his hands:*] *Do* something, do *something* . . . Intervene, move! . . .

ARCHITECT: [*calmly, still sitting, sandwich in hand, after another sip*] It's far too late now. Once again, he's taken us unawares . . .

BÉRENGER: Perhaps it's just a big stone he's thrown in the water . . . to tease us!

ARCHITECT: That *would* surprise me. And the cry?
  [*The* OWNER *comes in from the left.*]
  Now we'll know everything, anyway. Here comes our informer.

OWNER: It's the girl, the blonde one . . .

BÉRENGER: Dany? Mademoiselle Dany? It can't be!

ARCHITECT: It is. Why not? She's my secretary, my ex-secretary. And I gave her fair warning not to leave my staff. She was safe there.

BÉRENGER: Oh God, God, God!

ARCHITECT: She was in the Civil Service! He doesn't attack the Service! But no, she wanted her 'liberty'! That'll teach her. She's found it now, her liberty. I was expecting this . . .

BÉRENGER: Oh God, oh God! Poor girl . . . She didn't have time to say Yes to me!

ARCHITECT: [*continuing*] I was even sure it would happen! Unless she'd gone right out of the district as soon as she left the Service.

BÉRENGER: Mademoiselle Dany! Mademoiselle Dany! Mademoiselle Dany! [*Lamentation.*]

ARCHITECT: [*continuing*] Ah! People are so determined to have their own way, and above all the victims are so determined to revisit the scene of the crime! That's how they get caught!

BÉRENGER: [*almost sobbing*] Ooh! Monsieur Superintendent. Monsieur Superintendent, it's Mademoiselle Dany, Mademoiselle Dany! [*He crumples up on his chair, in a state of collapse.*]

ARCHITECT: [*to* OWNER] Make the usual report, routine, you know. [*He takes his telephone from his pocket:*] Hullo? . . . Hullo? . . . Another one . . . It's a young woman . . . Dany . . . the one who worked with us . . . No one caught in the act . . . Just suspicions . . . the same ones . . . yes! . . . One moment! [*He lays the telephone on the table.*]

BÉRENGER: [*suddenly jumps to his feet*] We can't, we mustn't let things go on like this! It's got to stop! It's got to stop!

ARCHITECT: Control yourself. We've all got to die. Let the investigation take its usual course!

BÉRENGER: [*runs off, slamming the imaginary shop-door with a bang, which is, however, heard*] It can't go on! We must *do* something! We must, we must, we must! [*He goes off right.*]

OWNER: Au revoir, Monsieur! [*To* ARCHITECT:] He might say goodbye!

ARCHITECT: [*still seated, he watches him go, like the* OWNER, *who is standing with his arms folded or his hands on his hips; then, as soon as* BÉRENGER *has gone, the* ARCHITECT *tosses off the rest of his wine and pointing to* BÉRENGER's *full glass says to the* OWNER] Drink it! Eat the sandwich too!

[*The* OWNER *sits down in* BÉRENGER's *place. On the telephone:*]

Hullo! No evidence! Close the case! Crime unsolved! [*He puts the telephone back in his pocket.*]

OWNER: [*drinking*] Santé! [*He bites into the sandwich.*]

CURTAIN

ACT TWO

BÉRENGER's *room. Dark and low-ceilinged, but lighter in the centre opposite the window. Near this long low window a chest. To the right of it a gloomy recess; in this dark patch an armchair French Regency style, rather knocked about, in which, as the curtain rises,* ÉDOUARD *is sitting, silently. At the begin-*

*ning of the Act he is not visible, nor is the armchair, because of
the darkness that reigns in* BÉRENGER'S *ground-floor room.*

*In the centre, in the brightest part, a large table in front of the
window, with notebooks and papers, a book, an inkstand and a
fancy penholder like a goose-quill.*

*A red worn-out armchair with one arm missing is a few feet to
the left of the table. In the left-hand wall, more shadowy corners.*

*In the rest of the room you can make out in the half-light the
shapes of old pieces of furniture: an old writing-desk and a
chest of drawers with a threadbare tapestry on the wall above it;
there is also a chair and another red armchair. Next to the
window, on the right, a small table, a footstool and some
shelves with a few books. On the top an old gramophone.*

*At the front of the stage on the left is the door that gives on the
landing. Hanging from the ceiling an old chandelier: on the
floor a faded old carpet. On the right-hand wall a mirror in a
baroque frame, which shines so little at the beginning of the act
that it is difficult to tell what the object is. Beneath the mirror
an old chimney-piece.*

*The curtains are not drawn, and through the window you can
see the street, the windows of the ground floor opposite and a
part of the front of a grocer's shop.*

*The décor of Act II is very much constructed, heavy, realistic
and ugly; it contrasts strongly with the lack of décor and the
simple lighting effects of Act I.*

*When the curtain rises the window lights the middle of the
stage and the central table with a pale yellowish light. The
walls of the house opposite are a dirty grey colour. Outside the
weather is dull; it is half snowing, half drizzling.*

Sitting in the armchair in the darkest corner of BÉRENGER'S
room, to the right of the window, ÉDOUARD *is neither seen nor
heard at the start of the Act. He will be seen later, after*

BÉRENGER's *arrival: thin, very pale, feverish-looking, dressed in black, with a mourning band round his right arm, a black felt hat, black overcoat, black shoes, white shirt with starched collar and black tie. Now and again, but only after* BÉRENGER's *arrival,* ÉDOUARD *will cough or clear his throat; from time to time he spits into a great white handkerchief with a black border, which he fastidiously returns to his pocket.*

A few moments before the rise of the curtain the VOICE OF THE CONCIERGE *is already heard coming from the left, that is from the landing in the block of flats.*

CONCIERGE: [*singing*] When it's cold it's not hot,
When it's hot, it's because it's cold!

Oh dear, you can sweep as much as you like, it's dirty all day long, what with their snow and their coal dust.
[*Noise of a broom knocking against the door, then the* CONCIERGE *is heard singing again:*]
When it's cold it's not hot,
When it's hot it's because it's cold,
When it's cold, it can't be hot!
When it's hot, how can it be cold?
What *is* it then when it's cold?
Cold as cold, and that's your lot!

[*During the song of the* CONCIERGE *there are sounds of hammering from the floor above, a radio blaring and trucks and motorcycles approaching and dying away; at one point too the shouts of children in the schoolyard during recreation: all this must be slightly distorted, caricatured, so the cries of the schoolchildren sound lik dogs yapping; the idea is to make the uproar sound worse, but in a way that is partly unpleasant and partly comic.*]

MAN'S VOICE: [*preceded by the noise of footsteps on the stairs and the barking of a dog*] Good morning, Madame la Concierge.

VOICE OF CONCIERGE: Good morning, Monsieur Lelard! You're late leaving this morning!

MAN'S VOICE: I've had some work to do at home. I've been asleep. Feel better now. Going to post my letters.

VOICE OF CONCIERGE: You've a funny sort of job! Always working with papers! Writing all those letters, you must have to think all the time.

MAN'S VOICE: It's not writing them that makes me think, but sending them off.

VOICE OF CONCIERGE: Yes, you've got to know who to send them to! Can't send them to *anyone*! Mustn't send them all to the same person, eh?

MAN'S VOICE: Still, got to earn your living by the sweat of your brow, as the prophet says.

VOICE OF CONCIERGE: There's too much education these days, that's where things go wrong. Take sweeping, even that's not as easy as it used to be.

MAN'S VOICE: Still, got to earn your living anyway, to pay your income tax.

VOICE OF CONCIERGE: Minister in Parliament, that's the best job. They don't *pay* taxes, they *collect* them.

MAN'S VOICE: Even poor chaps like them have to earn their living, just like anyone else.

VOICE OF CONCIERGE: Yes, the rich are probably as poor as us, if there's any left these days.

MAN'S VOICE: Ah yes, that's life.

VOICE OF CONCIERGE: Ah yes, afraid so!

MAN'S VOICE: Ah yes, Madame.

VOICE OF CONCIERGE: Ah yes, Monsieur. It's a dog's life, and we all end up in the same place, a hole in the ground. That's where my husband is, forty years ago he died, and it's just like yesterday. [*A dog barks at the entrance.*] Shut up, Treasure. [*She must have clouted the dog with her broom, for you can hear his plaintive yelps. A door bangs.*] Go back in. [*To the* MAN *presumably:*] Oh well, goodbye Monsieur Lelard. Careful now, it's slippery outside, the pavements are all wet. Stinking weather!

MAN'S VOICE: I'll say it is. We were talking about life, Madame, we've got to be philosophical, you know!

VOICE OF CONCIERGE: Don't you talk to me about philosophers! I once got it into my head to be all stoical and go in for meditation. They never taught me anything, even that Marcus Aurelius. Doesn't really do any good. We know as much as he does. We all have to find our own way out. If there was one, but there isn't.

MAN'S VOICE: Ah yes! . . .

VOICE OF CONCIERGE: And do without feelings too, how are we meant to find room for them? They don't enter into our account of things. How would feelings help *me* sweep my staircase?

MAN'S VOICE: I haven't read the philosophers.

VOICE OF CONCIERGE: You haven't missed much. That's what comes of being educated like you. Philosophy's no good except to put in a test-tube. May turn it a pretty colour, if you're lucky!

MAN'S VOICE: You shouldn't say that.

VOICE OF CONCIERGE: Philosophers! They're no good, except for a concierge like me.

MAN'S VOICE: You shouldn't say that, Madame, they're good for everyone.

VOICE OF CONCIERGE: I know what I'm talking about. You, you only read *good* books. I read the *philosophers*, because I've no money, the twopenny halfpenny philosophers. You, even if you've no money either, at least you can go to a library. You've got books to *choose* from . . . and what's the good of it, I ask you, you ought to know.

MAN'S VOICE: Philosophy, I say, is good for learning a philosophy of life!

VOICE OF CONCIERGE: I know all about the philosophy of life.

MAN'S VOICE: Good for you, Madame!

[*The broom knocks against the bottom of the door of* BÉREN-GER'*s room.*]

VOICE OF CONCIERGE: Oh dear, oh dear, what a dirty house this is! It's the slush!

MAN'S VOICE: Plenty of that about. Oh well, I'm off this time, time's pressing on. Au revoir, Madame, keep smiling.

VOICE OF CONCIERGE: Thanks, Monsieur Lelard! [*The entrance door is banged violently.*] Oh, that's clever of him, silly fool will smash the door next, and *I'll* have to pay for it!

MAN'S VOICE: [*politely*] Did you say something, Madame?

VOICE OF CONCIERGE: [*more politely still, sweetly*] It's nothing, Monsieur Lelard, just chatting to myself, learning to talk! Makes the time go quicker!

[*The broom knocks against the bottom of the door of* BÉREN-GER'*s room.*]

MAN'S VOICE: I quite thought you'd called me. Sorry.

VOICE OF CONCIERGE: Oh well, we all make mistakes, you know, Monsieur! Can't help it! No harm done. [*The front door is slammed violently again.*] He's gone this time. Tell him the same thing over and over again, he doesn't listen, him and his doors. Anybody'd think he was deaf! Likes to pretend he is, but he can hear all right! [*She sings:*]
When it's cold, it's not hot.

[*Yapping of the dog, more muffled.*] Shut up, Treasure! Ah, call that a dog! You wait, I'll knock hell out of you! [*You can hear the door of the* CONCIERGE'*s room opening. The dog yelps. The same door bangs again.*]

ANOTHER MAN'S VOICE: [*after the sound of footsteps: slightly*

foreign accent] Good morning, Madame la Concierge!
Mademoiselle Colombine, she live here?

VOICE OF CONCIERGE: Can't say I know the name! There
aren't any foreigners in the house. Only French people.

SECOND MAN: [*at the same time the upstairs radio is turned up
very loud*] But they told me she live on fifth floor this block.

VOICE OF CONCIERGE: [*shouting to make herself heard*] Can't
say I know the name, I tell you!

SECOND MAN'S VOICE: Please, Madame? [*Coming from the
street on the right, the lumbering sound of a truck, which suddenly
brakes a few seconds later.*]

VOICE OF CONCIERGE: [*still shouting*] I tell you I don't know
the name!

SECOND MAN'S VOICE: This Number Thirteen, Twelfth
Street?

VOICE OF CONCIERGE: [*as before*] What Street?

SECOND MAN'S VOICE: [*louder*] This Number Thirteen . . .

VOICE OF CONCIERGE: [*yelling*] Don't shout so loud. I can
hear you. Of course it's Number Thirteen, Twelfth Street.
Can't you read? It's written up outside.

SECOND MAN'S VOICE: Then it must be here Mademoiselle
Colombine lives!

TRUCK DRIVER'S VOICE: [*in the street*] Goddam learn to
drive!

VOICE OF CONCIERGE: I know better than you.

CAR DRIVER'S VOICE: [*in the street*] Don't you goddam
me!

VOICE OF CONCIERGE: Oh, I see, Mademoiselle Colombine,
perhaps you mean Monsieur Lecher's concubine?

TRUCK DRIVER'S VOICE: [*in the street*] Bastard! Pimp!

SECOND MAN'S VOICE: Yes, that's it! Latcher!

VOICE OF CONCIERGE: Latcher, Lecher, it's all the same!

CAR DRIVER: [*in the street*] Can't you be polite, damn you?

VOICE OF CONCIERGE: So it's the redhead you're after! If she's the one, *she* lives here, I told you she did! You want to say what you mean! Take the elevator!

TRUCK DRIVER: [*in the street*] Son of a bitch!

CAR DRIVER: [*in the street*] Son of a bitch, yourself. [*Combined noises of the elevator going up, the radio, vehicles starting up again in the street, and then the splutter of a motorbike; for a split second you can see the motorcyclist through the window, passing in the street*].

VOICE OF CONCIERGE: [*loudly*] Don't forget to shut the elevator door after you! [*To herself:*] They always forget, especially foreigners! [*She sings:*]

Of course you never get on, if you stay in the same place,
But do you really get on, if you're always changing places?
[*The door of the* CONCIERGE's *flat is heard banging; she has gone in: the dog yaps, her voice is more muffled:*] Yes, come on, my little Treasure! Who hasn't had his lump of sugar? Here it is, here's your sugar for you! [*Yapping.*] Take that! [*The dog howls. In the street two people can be seen through the window, coming on from the left. Or possibly you just hear them talking, without seeing them. Two* OLD MEN, *both decrepit, who hobble along painfully, taking small steps and leaning on their sticks.*]

1ST O.M.: Terrible weather.

2ND O.M.: Terrible weather.

1ST O.M.: What you say?

2ND O.M.: Terrible weather. What *you* say?

1ST O.M.: I said: terrible weather.

2ND O.M.: Hang on to my arm, you might slip over.

1ST O.M.: Hang on to my arm, you might slip over.

2ND O.M.: I used to know some surprising people, very surprising.

CLOCHARD: [*appearing from the right on the pavement opposite:*

he is singing:] When I left the Merchant Navy. [*He looks up at the windows; some coins could be thrown down.*]

1ST O.M.: What did they do, these surprising people?

2ND O.M.: They surprised everyone!

CLOCHARD: I got spliced to young Octavie!

1ST O.M.: And where did these surprising people surprise? [*The* CLOCHARD *does as before.*]

2ND O.M.: They surprised in society circles . . . everywhere they surprised!

1ST O.M.: When did you know them, these surprising people?

CLOCHARD: [*as before*] When I left the Merchant Navy . . . [*Still looking up at the windows of the upper floors, he makes off left and disappears.*]

2ND O.M.: In the old days, the old days . . .

1ST O.M.: Do you still see them sometimes?

GROCER: [*coming out of the shop opposite, looking furious and gazing up at a first-floor window*] Hey Madame!

2ND O.M.: Ah, my dear chap, there aren't any more nowadays, there aren't any more people who surprise . . . [*He is seen disappering on the right, and you can hear:*] All that's gone. I only know two of them today . . . two surprising people . . .

GROCER: Hey Madame! Who do you take me for?

2ND O.M.: . . . only two. One of them's retired and the other's deceased. [*The* 1ST OLD MAN *disappears too.*]

GROCER: [*as before*] I mean . . . who do you take me for?

VOICE OF CLOCHARD: [*singing*] The Captain of the tanker.

GROCER: [*as before*] Who do you take me for? I'm a shopkeeper, Madame, not a ragman! [*He goes furiously back to his shop.*]

VOICE OF CLOCHARD: [*moving away*]

Sent for me and said

If you want to get spliced to young Octavie
You'd better leave the Merchant Navy . . .

VOICE OF IST O.M.: [*moving away*] If there were any, you wouldn't notice. Surprising people don't surprise any more.

[*From the right the noise of recreation, which has already been heard quietly, redoubles in intensity. A schoolbell rings.*]

SCHOOLMASTER VOICE: Back to class! Back to class!

VOICE FROM THE STREET: We've fifty-eight delivery boys . . .

SCHOOLMASTER VOICE: Silence! [*Stamping of feet, shouting, noise of desks, etc., from the right.*] Silence! Silence!

VOICE FROM THE STREET: We've fifty-eight delivery boys! [*The children in the school are silent.*]

SCHOOLMASTER VOICE: History lesson: the people's representatives came to the gates of the palace of Queen Marie Antoinette. And they shouted . . .

VOICE FROM THE STREET: We've fifty-eight delivery boys!

SCHOOLMASTER VOICE: They shouted: we haven't any more cake, Your Majesty, give us cake. There isn't any left, replied the Queen.

VOICE FROM THE STREET: We've fifty-eight delivery boys!

SCHOOLMASTER VOICE: There isn't any left, why don't you eat bread? Then the people grew angry and cut off the Queen's head. When the Queen saw that she'd lost her head, she was so upset she had a stroke. She couldn't get over it, whatever the doctors did. They weren't up to much at the time.

VOICE FROM THE STREET: We've fifty-eight delivery boys!

GRUFF VOICE: [*in the street*] We were seven thousand feet up, when suddenly I saw the wing of our plane coming off.

ANOTHER VOICE: [*thin and piping*] You don't say!

GRUFF VOICE: All right, I said to myself, we've still got one

left. The passengers all piled up on one side of the plane
to keep an even keel and it went flying on with one wing.

PIPING VOICE: Were you frightened?

GRUFF VOICE: You wait . . . suddenly the second wing fell
off, and then the engines . . . and the propellers . . . and
we were seven thousand feet up!

PIPING VOICE: Phew!

GRUF VOICE: This time I thought we'd had it . . . [*The voice
fades:*] Really had it, no way out . . . Well, do you know
what saved us? Give you three guesses . . .

VOICE FROM THE STREET: Our fifty-eight delivery boys
waste too much time urinating. Five times a day, on
average, they interrupt their deliveries to satisfy a personal
need. The time is not deducted from their wages. They
take advantage of this, so they've got to be disciplined;
they can make water in turn once a month for four and a
half hours without interruption. That will save all the
coming and going, which sends up our costs. After all,
camels store up water.

1ST VOICE FROM BELOW: I went to catch my train, find my
compartment and sit down in my reserved seat. The train
was about to leave. Just at that minute in comes a gentleman with the same seat and the same number as me. Out
of politeness I gave up my seat and went and stood in the
corridor. He hardly said thank you. I stood for two hours.
In the end the train stopped at a station and the man got
off. I went and sat down again, as the seat was mine in the
first place. Again the train pulled out. An hour later it
stopped at another station. And the same man gets in
again and wants his seat back! Legally had he any right
to it? It was my seat as well as his, but he claimed second
occupant's rights. We went to law about it. The judge
said the man was entitled to extra privileges, because he

was a blue-blooded critic,[1] and it was only modesty made him conceal his identity.

ANOTHER VOICE FROM BELOW: Who was the gentleman?

1ST VOICE: A national hero. Harold Hastings de Hobson.[1]

2ND VOICE: How did he manage to catch the same train again?

1ST VOICE: He took a short cutting.

VOICE FROM THE STREET: [*closer*] We've fifty-eight delivery boys.

[*The two* OLD MEN *reappear in the street from the opposite direction, that is from the left.*]

1ST O.M.: I was invited to the wedding reception, of course . . . I wasn't very satisfied because all I like is *coq au vin* . . .

2ND O.M.: They didn't serve any *coq au vin*?

1ST O.M.: They *did*. But they didn't tell me it was *coq au vin*, so it didn't taste right.

2ND O.M.: Was it really *coq au vin*?

1ST O.M.: It WAS *coq au vin*, but as I didn't know, the whole meal was a farce.

2ND O.M.: I wish I'd been invited instead of you. I *like* my dishes *farcis*. [*They go off.*]

VOICE FROM THE STREET: We've fifty-eight delivery boys!

VOICE FROM RIGHT: We must seriously raise the question of our finances.

VOICE FROM ABOVE: Has the problem been considered by the delegation of deputy delegates?

VOICE FROM LEFT: We must seriously raise the question of *their* finances.

---

[1] There is a pun here in the original on the name of the French writer and dramatic critic, Morvan Lebesque. Harold Hobson is a natural choice in England for his well known admiration of French drama. American readers might like to pun on the name of an American critic.
Tr.

VOICE FROM ABOVE: We must seriously raise the question of the finances of our delivery boys.

ANOTHER VOICE FROM LEFT: No, the problem's been solved by the delegate of the deputy delegation.

VOICE FROM RIGHT: After all, production is production! The whole basis of the problem must be re-examined.

VOICE FROM LEFT: With our overseers and our underseers, our visionaries and our viewfinders, we shall form an organizational basis, a common funds committee.

VOICE FROM ABOVE: The seers and the underseers will form development committees for companies of contractors who will form special communities . . .

VOICE FROM RIGHT: There's the basic organizational principle and the organizational aspect of the superstructure.

VOICE FROM LEFT: What about our fifty-eight delivery boys?

VOICE FROM ABOVE: After work, we must organize leisure.

VOICE FROM BELOW: Concentrated leisure.

VOICE FROM LEFT: We must force the pace of leisure.

[*For some seconds thick fog darkens the stage: for a while the sounds from outside are muffled, all you can hear are vague snatches of dialogue.*]

VOICE OF CONCIERGE: [*after a banging of doors in the entrance*] Oh, when the fog's mixed with the factory smoke, you can't hear a word! [*Strident whistle from a factory hooter.*] Thank God for the hooters!

[*The fog has lifted, and on the other side of the street, you can see the* CLOCHARD *singing:*]

CLOCHARD: The second in command
      Sent for me and told me
      To marry my Octavie
      To marry my Octavie

[*The street sounds fade a little to facilitate the following scene.*]

And I'd be as good a slavey
As I'd once been in the Navy!
[*In the entrance a door is heard banging, while the* CLOCHARD, *still singing, looks up at the windows to catch the coins as they fall, takes off his battered old hat in general acknowledgment and comes nearer the window, advancing into the middle of the street.*]

VOICE OF CONCIERGE: Don't bang the door like that!

WOMAN'S VOICE: [*in entrance*] You bang it too sometimes. I didn't mean to.

VOICE OF CONCIERGE: Yes, but with me it's because I don't know when I'm doing it.

CLOCHARD: [*in the street, looking up at the windows*] Thank you, ladies and gentlemen, thank you! [*He starts muttering when there are no coins falling.*] They're a stingy lot, curse 'em!

VOICE OF CONCIERGE: [*singing*] Cold as cold
And that's your lot.

CLOCHARD: [*while the* CONCIERGE *goes on singing the same refrain, he has crossed the street. A motorcyclist brushes past him from behind, travelling fast, and a voice is heard: 'Stupid bastard'*] As I'd once been in the Navy! [*He is right up to the window, and as he sings:*

But keep a weather eye,
But keep a weather eye! . . .

he looks through the window into BÉRENGER'*s room, squashing his face and nose up against the glass.*]

CONCIERGE: [*making her appearance on the pavement, which she is sweeping, singing away until she bumps into the* CLOCHARD] What are you doing here?

CLOCHARD: I'm singing!

CONCIERGE: You're dirtying the window panes! That's one of my tenants', and I'm the one has to keep them clean.

CLOCHARD: [*sarcastically*] Oh! I beg your pardon, Madame.
I didn't know. No need to get upset.

CONCIERGE: Go on, clear off and don't be a nuisance!

CLOCHARD: [*still a bit cheeky and rather drunk*] I've heard that
a thousand times before. You're not very original,
Madame.

CONCIERGE: [*threatening him with her broom*] I'll teach you to
play the critic with me.

CLOCHARD: Don't trouble yourself, Madame, I'm going,
Madame, I'm sorry! [*He moves off, still singing:*]

When I left the Merchant Navy
I got spliced to young Octavie.

CONCIERGE: [*still in the street near the window, she wheels round
as the dog barks*] Shut up! . . . The postman! [*To the* POST-
MAN:] Who's it for, Postman?

POSTMAN'S VOICE: Telegram for Monsieur Bérenger!

CONCIERGE: Ground floor, on the right.

POSTMAN'S VOICE: Thanks.

CONCIERGE: [*waving her broom after the* CLOCHARD, *who is no
longer visible*] Lazy old bugger! [*Shrugging her shoulders:*]
If he's a sailor, I'm a tart!

[*The* POSTMAN *is heard knocking at* BÉRENGER'*s door, while
the* CONCIERGE *sweeps the pavement.*]

Oh, all this dog's mess, I wouldn't let mine do it.

POSTMAN'S VOICE: No reply.

CONCIERGE: [*to invisible* POSTMAN] Knock louder. He's
there.

POSTMAN'S VOICE: I tell you there's no reply.

CONCIERGE: Don't even know how to knock on a door! [*She
disappears into the entrance.*] Of course he can't have gone
out, I ought to know his habits. He is my tenant. I even
do his housework. Clean his windows!

POSTMAN'S VOICE: Try!

[*Loud knocking is heard, repeated several times, on* BÉREN-GER's *door.*]

VOICE OF CONCIERGE: [*knocking at the door*] Monsieur Bérenger! Monsieur Bérenger! [*Silence, then more knocking.*] Monsieur Bérenger! Monsieur Bérenger!

POSTMAN'S VOICE: What did I tell you!

VOICE OF CONCIERGE: Well, I like that! He can't have gone out. Could be asleep, but that's not one of his habits! Knock louder! I'll go and look!

[*The* POSTMAN *goes on knocking and the* CONCIERGE *appears again outside the window; she glues her face to the window pane. Her face is naturally hideous, but with her nose squashed against the glass it looks even worse.*]

CONCIERGE: Monsieur Bérenger! I say, Monsieur Bérenger!

[*At the same time the* POSTMAN *is heard knocking at the door.*]

POSTMAN'S VOICE: Monsieur Bérenger! Telegram, Monsieur Bérenger!

CONCIERGE: Monsieur Bérenger, there's a telegram for you . . . fine state of affairs! [*Pause.*] Where on earth can he be? He's never at home! [*She raps on the window again, while the* POSTMAN's *knocking continues.*] Some people go for walks, got nothing better to do, and we work our fingers to the bone! . . . He's not there! [*She disappears: she must be near the entrance as you can see her arm brandishing the broom out of once corner of the window.*]

POSTMAN'S VOICE: If he's not in, he's not in. And you said he never went out!

VOICE OF CONCIERGE: I didn't! Give me the telegram, I'll give it to him! [*She disappears completely.*] I'm the one cleans his windows!

POSTMAN'S VOICE: I'm not allowed to give it to you. I can't.

VOICE OF CONCIERGE: That's that, then, keep it.

POSTMAN'S VOICE: I'll give it you anyway. Here it is.

CONCIERGE: Now I've got to keep a look-out for him! Oh dear!

[*Pause. The noises have suddenly ceased, after the dying fall of one last factory siren. Perhaps too the* CONCIERGE *has been heard for one last time abusing her dog, which yelps as usual. A few moments' silence. Then, passing along the street close to the window,* BÉRENGER *can be seen coming home. He has his overcoat on and is clutching his hat in his right hand; he is swinging his arm vigorously. He is walking with his head down. Once he has gone past the window his steps are heard in the entrance. Then his key turns in the lock.*]

VOICE OF CONCIERGE: [*very polite*] Why, it's you, Monsieur Bérenger! Had a nice walk? You need some fresh air! Good idea!

VOICE OF BÉRENGER: Good morning, Madame.

VOICE OF CONCIERGE: If you've been for a walk, you must have gone out. Didn't hear you go. Why didn't you tell me, I hadn't got a key to do your room. How could I know? *I* was ready. Telegram came for you.

[*Pause.* BÉRENGER *has stopped opening the door to read the telegram.*]

I hope it wasn't urgent? I read it, you see. It's the old clothes man. Wants you, urgently. Nothing to worry about.

[*The key is again heard grating in the lock. The door of* BÉRENGER'*s room opens quietly. The* CONCIERGE *is heard angrily muttering words that are indistinguishable, then she bangs the door of her flat and the dog squeals. The figure of* BÉRENGER *can be picked out in the dim room. He advances slowly towards the centre of the stage. The silence is complete. He turns the electric light switch and the stage lights up.* ÉDOUARD *is seen in his corner, with his hat on his head, wearing his overcoat, his briefcase at his feet, clearing his throat. Surprised, first by the coughing, then almost at the same time by the sight of* ÉDOUARD *himself,* BÉRENGER *gives a jump.*]

BÉRENGER: Oh, what are you doing here?

ÉDOUARD: [*in a thin, rather high-pitched voice, almost childlike, as he gets up coughing, picking up his briefcase, which he keeps in his hand*] Your place isn't very warm. [*He spits into his handkerchief. To do this he has laid his briefcase down again and taken his right hand out of his pocket; this arm is slightly withered and visibly shorter than the other. Then, carefully and methodically, he folds up his handkerchief again, puts it back in his pocket and picks up his briefcase.*]

BÉRENGER: You startled me . . . I wasn't expecting you, what are you doing here?

ÉDOUARD: Waiting for you. [*Putting his deformed hand back in his pocket.*] How are you, Bérenger?

BÉRENGER: How did you get in?

ÉDOUARD: Through the door of course. I opened it.

BÉRENGER: How? I had the keys with me!

ÉDOUARD: [*taking some keys from his pocket and showing them to* BÉRENGER] So did I! [*He puts the keys back in his pocket.*]

BÉRENGER: How did you get those keys? [*He lays his hat on the table.*]

ÉDOUARD: But . . . you let me have them for a while yourself, so I could come to your flat when I liked, and wait for you if you were out.

BÉRENGER: [*trying to remember*] *I* gave you those keys? . . . When? . . . I don't remember at all . . .

ÉDOUARD: You gave them to me all the same. How else could I have got them?

BÉRENGER: Édouard, it's amazing. Still, if you say . . .

ÉDOUARD: I promise you did . . . I'm sorry, Bérenger, I'll give them back if you don't want me to have them.

BÉRENGER: Oh . . . no, no . . . keep them, Édouard, keep them now you've got them. I'm sorry, I've a bad memory. I don't remember giving them to you.

ÉDOUARD: Well, you did . . . you remember, it was last year, I think. One Sunday when . . .

BÉRENGER: [*interrupting him*] The concierge didn't tell me you were waiting.

ÉDOUARD: I don't suppose she saw me, it's my fault, I didn't know I had to ask *her* if I could come to your flat. I thought you told me it wasn't necessary. But if you don't want me here . . .

BÉRENGER: That's not what I mean. I'm always pleased to see you.

ÉDOUARD: I don't want to be in the way.

BÉRENGER: You know it's not that at all.

ÉDOUARD: Thanks.

BÉRENGER: It's losing my memory that upsets me . . . [*To himself:*] Still, the concierge oughtn't to have left the flats this morning! . . . [*To* ÉDOUARD:] What's wrong with you? You're trembling.

ÉDOUARD: Yes, I am. I don't feel very well. I'm cold.

BÉRENGER: [*taking the sound hand in his, while* ÉDOUARD *stuffs the other in his pocket*] You've still got a temperature. Coughing and shivering. You're very pale and your eyes look feverish.

ÉDOUARD: My lungs . . . they're not improving . . . after all the time I've had trouble with them . . .

BÉRENGER: And this building's so badly heated . . . [*Without taking his overcoat off he goes and sinks morosely into an armchair near the table, while* ÉDOUARD *remains standing.*] Do sit down, Édouard.

ÉDOUARD: Thank you, thanks very much. [*He sits down again on the chest, cautiously setting his briefcase down near him, within reach; he always seems to be keeping an eye on it. A moment's silence. Then, noticing how gloomy* BÉRENGER *is looking and how he is sighing:*] You seem so sad, you look worn out and anxious . . .

BÉRENGER: [*to himself*] If that was all . . .

ÉDOUARD: *You're* not ill too, are you? . . . What's wrong? Has something happened to you?

BÉRENGER: No, no . . . nothing at all. I'm like that . . . I'm not cheerful by nature! Brrr . . . I'm cold too! [*He rubs his hands.*]

ÉDOUARD: I'm sure something's happened to you. You're more nervous than usual, you're quite jumpy! Tell me about it, if I'm not being indiscreet, it may help.

BÉRENGER: [*getting up and taking a few excited paces in the room*] I've got good reason.

ÉDOUARD: What's wrong?

BÉRENGER: Oh, nothing, nothing and everything . . . everything . . .

ÉDOUARD: I should like a cup of tea, if I may . . .

BÉRENGER: [*suddenly adopting the serious tones of a tragic pronouncement*] My dear Édouard, I am shattered, in despair, inconsolable!

ÉDOUARD: [*without changing the tone of his voice*] Shattered by what, in despair about what?

BÉRENGER: My finacée has been murdered.

ÉDOUARD: I beg your pardon?

BÉRENGER: My fiancée has been murdered, do you hear?

ÉDOUARD: Your fiancée? Since when have you been engaged? You never told me you were thinking of getting married. Congratulations. My condolences too. Who was she?

BÉRENGER: To be honest . . . She wasn't exactly my fiancée . . . just a girl, a young girl who might have been.

ÉDUOUARD: Ah yes?

BÉRENGER: A girl who was as beautiful as she was sweet and tender, pure as an angel. It's terrible. Too terrible.

ÉDOUARD: How long had you known her?

BÉRENGER: Always, perhaps. Since this morning anyway.

ÉDOUARD: Quite recently.

BÉRENGER: She was snatched from me . . . snatched away! . . . I . . . [*Gesture of the hand.*]

ÉDOUARD: It must be very hard . . . please, have you any tea?

BÉRENGER: I'm sorry, I wasn't thinking . . . With this tragedy . . . which has ruined my life! Yes, I've got some.

ÉDOUARD: I understand.

BÉRENGER: You couldn't understand.

ÉDOUARD: Oh yes I do.

BÉRENGER: I can't offer you tea . . . It's gone mouldy. I'd forgotten.

ÉDOUARD: Well, a glass of rum, please . . . I'm quite numb with cold . . .

[BÉRENGER *produces a bottle of rum, fills a small glass for* ÉDOUARD *and offers it to him while he says:*]

BÉRENGER: No one will ever take her place. My life is over. It's a wound that will never heal.

ÉDOUARD: You really have been wounded, poor old thing! [*Taking the glass of rum.*] Thanks! [*Still in a tone of indifference:*] Poor old thing!

BÉRENGER: And if that was all, if there was nothing but the murder of that unfortunate girl. Do you know the things that happen in the world, awful things, in our town, terrible things, you can't imagine . . . quite near here . . . comparatively close . . . morally speaking it's actually here! [*He strikes his breast.* ÉDOUARD *has swallowed his rum, chokes and coughs.*] Aren't you feeling well?

ÉDOUARD: It's nothing. It's so strong. [*He goes on coughing.*] I must have swallowed it the wrong way.

BÉRENGER: [*gently hitting* ÉDOUARD *on the back to stop him coughing and with the other hand taking his glass from him*] I thought I'd found everything again, got it all back. [*To* ÉDOUARD:] Stretch your head up and look at the ceiling. It'll stop. [*He goes on:*] All I'd lost and all I hadn't lost, all that had been mine and all that had never been mine . . .

ÉDOUARD: [*to* BÉRENGER, *who is still hitting him on the back*] Thank you . . . that's enough . . . you're hurting . . . stop it, please.

BÉRENGER: [*going to place the little glass on the table while* ÉDOUARD *spits into his handkerchief*] I thought the spring had returned for ever . . . that I'd found the unfindable again, the dream, the key, life . . . all that we've lost while we've gone on living.

ÉDOUARD: [*clearing his throat*] Yes. Of course.

BÉRENGER: All our muddled aspirations, all the things we vaguely yearn for, from the depths of our being, without even realizing . . . Oh, I thought I'd found everything . . . It was unexplored territory, magically beautiful.

ÉDOUARD: The girl was unexplored? . . .

BÉRENGER: No. The place. The girl, if you like, too!

ÉDOUARD: You're always searching for something out of the way. Always aiming at something out of reach.

BÉRENGER: But I tell you it wasn't. This girl . . .

ÉDOUARD: The answer is that it *is*, and so is *she* now. Your problems are so complicated, so impractical. You've always been dissatisfied, always refused to resign yourself.

BÉRENGER: That's because I'm suffocating . . . The air I have to breathe is not the kind that's made for me.

ÉDOUARD: [*clearing his throat*] Think yourself lucky you don't suffer from ill-health, you're not a sick man or an invalid.

BÉRENGER: [*without paying attention to what* ÉDOUARD *is saying*]
No. No. I've seen it, I thought I'd got somewhere . . .
somewhere like a different universe. Yes, only beauty can
make the spring flowers bloom eternally . . . everlasting
flowers . . . but I'm sorry to say it was only a light that
lied! . . . Once again everything fell into chaos . . . in a
flash, in a flash! The same collapse, again and again . . .
[*All this is said in a declamatory tone half way between sincerity
and parody.*]

ÉDOUARD: You think only of yourself.

BÉRENGER: [*with slight irritation*] That's not true! Not true. I
don't just think of myself. It's not for myself . . . not only
for myself that I'm suffering right now, that I refuse to
accept things! There comes a time when they're too
horrible, and you can't . . .

ÉDOUARD: But that's the way of the world. Think of me, I'm
a sick man . . . I've come to terms . . .

BÉRENGER: [*interrupting him*] It weighs on you, it weighs on
you terribly, especially when you think you've seen . . .
when you've thought you could hope . . . Oh! . . . then
you can't go on . . . I'm tired . . . she's dead and they're
dead and they'll all be killed . . . no one can stop it.

ÉDOUARD: But how did she die, this fiancée who perhaps
wasn't? And who else is going to be killed, apart from the
ones who usually get killed? What in fact are you talking
about? Is it your dreams that are being killed? Generali-
ties don't mean a thing.

BÉRENGER: I'm not talking through my hat . . .

ÉDOUARD: I'm sorry. I just can't understand you. I don't . . .

BÉRENGER: You're always wrapped up in your own little
world. You never know anything. Where have you been
living?

ÉDOUARD: Tell me about it then, give me some details.

BÉRENGER: It's absolutely incredible. There is this in our town, though you're not aware of it, one beautiful district.

ÉDOUARD: Well?

BÉRENGER: Yes, there's one beautiful district. I've found it, I've just come from there. It's called the radiant city.

ÉDOUARD: Well, well!

BÉRENGER: In spite of it's name it's not a model neighbourhood, a happy or a perfect one. A criminal, an insatiable murderer, has turned it into hell.

ÉDOUARD: [*coughing*] I'm sorry, I can't help coughing!

BÉRENGER: You heard what I said?

ÉDOUARD: Perfectly: a murderer's turned it into hell.

BÉRENGER: He terrorizes and kills everyone. The district's getting deserted. It'll soon cease to exist.

ÉDOUARD: Oh yes, of course. I know! It must be that beggar who shows people the Colonel's photo and while they're looking at it throws them in the water! It's a trick to catch a fool. I thought you meant something else. If that's all it is . . .

BÉRENGER: [*surprised*] You knew? Knew all about it?

ÉDOUARD: Of course, I've known for a long time. I thought you were going to tell me something fresh, that there was another beautiful district.

BÉRENGER: Why did you never tell me anything about it?

ÉDOUARD: I didn't think there was any point. The whole town knows the story. I'm surprised even, you didn't know about it before, it's old news. Who doesn't know? . . . There didn't seem any need to tell you.

BÉRENGER: What? You mean everyone knows?

ÉDOUARD: That's what I said. You see, even *I* knew. It's a known fact, accepted and filed away. Even the schoolchildren know.

BÉRENGER: Even the schoolchildren? . . . Are you sure?

ÉDOUARD: Of course I am. [*He clears his throat.*]

BÉRENGER: How could children at school have found out? . . .

ÉDOUARD: Must have heard their parents talking . . . or grandparents . . . the schoolmaster too when he teaches them to read and write . . . Would you give me a little more rum? . . . Or perhaps not, it's so bad for me . . . I'd better go without. [*Taking up his explanation again:*] It's a pity, I agree.

BÉRENGER: A great pity! A terrible pity . . .

ÉDOUARD: What can we do about it?

BÉRENGER: Now it's my turn to say how very surprised *I* am to see you taking the matter so calmly . . . I always thought you were a sensitive, humane man.

ÉDOUARD: Perhaps I am.

BÉRENGER: But it's atrocious. Atrocious.

ÉDOUARD: I agree, I don't deny it.

BÉRENGER: Your indifference makes me sick! And I don't mind saying it to your face.

ÉDOUARD: Well you know . . . I . . .

BÉRENGER: [*louder*] Your indifference makes me sick!

ÉDOUARD: Don't forget . . . this is all new to you . . .

BÉRENGER: That's no excuse. You disappoint me, Édouard, frankly you disappoint me . . .

[ÉDOUARD *has a violent bout of coughing; he spits into his handkerchief.* BÉRENGER *rushes up to* ÉDOUARD, *who nearly collapses.*]

You're really ill.

ÉDOUARD: A glass of water.

BÉRENGER: At once. I'll go and fetch one. [*Supporting him.*] Lie down here . . . on the couch . . .

ÉDOUARD: [*between coughs*] My briefcase . . . [BÉRENGER *bends down to pick up* ÉDOUARD'S *briefcase. In spite of his state of collapse,* Édouard *springs away from* Bérenger *to get hold of himself.*] No . . . let me . . . [*He takes the briefcase from* Bérenger's *hand, then, still weak and supported by* Bérenger, *he reaches the couch, still clinging to the briefcase, and lies down with* Bérenger's *help, the briefcase at his side.*]

Bérenger: You're soaked in perspiration . . .

Édouard: And frozen stiff as well, oh . . . this cough . . . it's awful . . .

Bérenger: You mustn't catch cold. Would you like a blanket?

Édouard: [*shivering*] Don't worry. It's nothing . . . it'll pass . . .

Bérenger: Settle down and rest.

Édouard: A glass of water.

Bérenger: At once . . . I'll fetch one.

[*He hurries out to fetch a glass of water; you can hear the water running at the tap. Meanwhile* Édouard *raises himself on one elbow and stops coughing; with one anxious hand he checks the lock of his enormous black briefcase, and then, somewhat relieved, lies back again still coughing but not so loudly.* Édouard *must not give the impression he is trying to deceive* Bérenger: *he is really ill and he has other worries, his briefcase for example. He wipes his brow.* Bérenger *returns with the glass of water.*]

Feel better?

Édouard: Thanks . . . [*He takes a sip of the water and* Bérenger *takes the glass from him.*] I'm sorry, It's stupid of me. I'm all right now.

Bérenger: I'm the one to say I'm sorry. I should have realized . . . When you're ill yourself, when you're really a sick man, like you, it's hard to get carried away by something else . . . I've not been fair to you. After all, these terrible crimes in the radiant city might be the cause of your illness. It must have affected you, consciously or otherwise. Yes, I'm sure it's that that's eating you away. I confess it's wrong to pass judgment too lightly. You can't know people's hearts . . .

ÉDOUARD: [*getting up*] I'm freezing here . . .

BÉRENGER: Don't get up. I'll go and fetch a blanket.

ÉDOUARD: I'd rather we went for a little walk, for the fresh air. I waited for you too long in this cold. I'm sure it's warmer outside.

BÉRENGER: I'm so tired emotionally, so depressed. I'd rather have gone to bed . . . Still, if that's what you really want, I don't mind coming with you for a while!

ÉDOUARD: That's very charitable of you!

[*ÉDOUARD puts his black-ribboned felt hat on again, buttons his dark overcoat and dusts it down, while BÉRENGER also puts his hat on. ÉDOUARD picks up his heavy, bulging black briefcase. BÉRENGER walks in front of him, turning his back to ÉDOUARD, who, as he passes the table, lifts the briefcase over it. As he does so, the briefcase opens and a part of the contents spill over the table: at first, large photographs.*]

My briefcase!

BÉRENGER: [*turning round at the noise*] What the . . . ah!

[*They both make a quick movement to the briefcase at the same time.*]

ÉDOUARD: Leave it to me.

BÉRENGER: No, wait, I'll help you . . . [*He sees the photos.*] But . . . but . . . what have you got there?

[*He picks up one of the photos. ÉDOUARD tries, but without appearing too alarmed, to take it back from him, to hide the other photos falling from his briefcase with his hands, and push them back. BÉRENGER, who has held on to the photo, looks at it in spite of ÉDOUARD's opposition.*]

What is it?

E   129

ÉDOUARD: I expect it's a photo . . . some photos . . .

BÉRENGER: [*still holding the photo and inspecting it*] It's an army man, with a moustache and pips . . . A Colonel with his decorations, the Military Cross . . . [*He picks up other photos.*] More photos! And always the same face.

ÉDOUARD: [*also looking*] Yes . . . it is . . . it's a Colonel. [*He seems to be trying to lay his hands on the photos; meanwhile a lot of others keep on pouring over the table.*]

BÉRENGER: [*with authority*] Let me see! [*He dives into the brief-case, pulls out more photos and looks at one:*] Quite a nice face. With the kind of expression that makes you feel sorry for him. [*He takes out more photos.* ÉDOUARD *mops his brow.*] What *is* all this? Why, it's the photo, the famous photo of the Colonel! You had it in there . . . you never told me!

ÉDOUARD: I'm not always looking inside my briefcase!

BÉRENGER: But it *is* your briefcase all right, you're never without it.

ÉDOUARD: That's no reason . . .

BÉRENGER: Oh well . . . We'll take the opporutnity, while we're at it, of having another look!

[BÉRENGER *sticks his hands into the huge black briefcase.* ÉDOUARD *does the same with his own too-white hand, whose twisted fingers are now very clearly visible.*]

More photos of the Colonel . . . and more . . . and more . . . [*To* ÉDOUARD, *who is now taking things out of the briefcase too, and looking astonished:*] What are these?

ÉDOUARD: You can see, they're artificial flowers.

BÉRENGER: There are masses of them! . . . And these . . . Look, dirty pictures . . . [*He inspects them while* ÉDOUARD *goes and looks over his shoulder:*] Nasty!

ÉDOUARD: Excuse me! [*He takes a step away.*]

BÉRENGER: [*discarding the obscene photos and continuing his inventory*] Some sweets . . . money-boxes . . . [*They both take from the briefcase a heterogeneous collection of articles.*] . . . children's watches! . . . What are they doing here?

ÉDOUARD: [*stammering*] I . . . I don't know . . . I tell you . . .

BÉRENGER: What do you make of it?

ÉDOUARD: Nothing. What *can* you make of it?

BÉRENGER: [*still taking from the briefcase, which is like a conjuror's bottomless bag, an amazing quantity of all types of objects, which cover the whole surface of the table and even fall on the floor*] . . . pins . . . and more pins . . . pen-holders . . . and these . . . and these . . . what's that?

[*Much should be made of this scene: some of the objects can fly away on their own, others can be thrown by* BÉRENGER *to the four corners of the stage.*]

ÉDOUARD: That? . . . I don't know . . . I don't know at all . . . I know nothing about it.

BÉRENGER: [*showing him a box*] What on earth's this?

ÉDOUARD: [*taking it in his hand*] Looks to me like a box, isn't it?

BÉRENGER: It is. A cardboard box. What's inside?

ÉDOUARD: I don't know. I don't know. I couldn't tell you.

BÉRENGER: Open it, go on, open it.

ÉDOUARD: [*almost indifferently*] If you like . . . [*He opens the box.*] Nothing there! Oh yes, another box . . . [*He takes the small box out.*]

BÉRENGER: And that box?

ÉDOUARD: See for yourself.

BÉRENGER: [*taking a third box from the second box*] Another box. [*He looks into the third box.*] Inside there's another box. [*He takes it out.*] And another inside that . . . [*He looks into the fourth box.*] And another box inside that . . . and so on, ad infinitum! Let's look again . . .

ÉDOUARD: Oh, if you want . . . But it'll stop us going for a walk . . .

BÉRENGER: [*taking boxes out*] Box . . . after box . . . after box
. . . after box . . . after box . . . !

ÉDOUARD: Nothing but boxes . . .

BÉRENGER: [*taking a handful of cigarettes from the briefcase*]
Cigarettes!

ÉDOUARD: Those belong to me! [*He starts collecting them, then
stops.*] Take one if you like . . .

BÉRENGER: Thanks, I don't smoke.

> [ÉDOUARD *puts a handful of cigarettes in his pocket, while
> others scatter over the table and fall on the floor.* BÉRENGER
> *stares at* ÉDOUARD:]

These things belong to that monster! You had them in
here!

ÉDOUARD: I didn't know, I didn't know about it! [*He goes
to take the briefcase back.*]

BÉRENGER: No, no. Empty it all! Go on!

ÉDOUARD: It makes me tired. You can do it yourself, but I
don't see what use it is. [*He passes him the gaping briefcase.*]

BÉRENGER: [*taking another box out*] It's only another box.

ÉDOUARD: I told you.

BÉRENGER: [*looking inside the empty briefcase*] There's nothing
else.

ÉDOUARD: Can I put the things back? [*He begins picking up
the objects and putting them back in the briefcase, higgledy-
piggledy.*]

BÉRENGER: The monster's things! Those are the monster's
things. It's extraordinary . . .

ÉDOUARD: [*as before*] Er . . . yes . . . there's no denying it . . .
It's true.

BÉRENGER: How do they come to be in your briefcase?

ÉDOUARD: Really . . . I . . . What do you expect me to say?
. . . You can't always explain everything . . . May I put
them back?

BÉRENGER: I suppose so, yes, why not . . . What good could they be to us? [*He begins helping* ÉDOUARD *to fill the brief-case with the things he has taken out; then suddenly, as he is about to put back the last box, the one he did not examine, it opens and scatters over the table all kinds of documents as well as several dozen visiting cards. All this is in the style of a conjuring trick.*] Look, visiting cards.

ÉDOUARD: Yes. Visiting cards. So they are, how amazing . . . well I never!

BÉRENGER: [*inspecting the visiting cards*] That must be his name . . .

ÉDOUARD: Whose name?

BÉRENGER: The criminal's name, of course, the criminal's name!

ÉDOUARD: You think so?

BÉRENGER: It seems obvious to me.

ÉDOUARD: Really, why?

BÉRENGER: You can see for yourself, can't you! All the visiting cards have the same name. Look and read! [*He offers* ÉDOUARD *a few of the cards.*]

ÉDOUARD: [*reading the name written on the cards*] You're right . . . the same name . . . the same name on them all . . . It's quite true!

BÉRENGER: Ah . . . but . . . my dear Édouard, this is getting more and more peculiar, yes, [*Looking at him:*] more and more peculiar!

ÉDOUARD: You don't think . . .

BÉRENGER: [*taking the objects he mentions from the box*] And here's his address . . .

[ÉDOUARD *gently clears his throat, appearing slightly worried.*]

And his identity card . . . photo of him! . . . It's him all right . . . His own photo clipped to the Colonel's. [*With growing excitement:*] An address book . . . with the names and addresses . . . of all his victims! . . . We'll catch him, Édouard, we'll catch him!

ÉDOUARD: [*suddenly producing a neat little box; he could take it from his pocket or from one of his sleeves, like a conjuror, a folding box perhaps, which he flicks into shape as he shows it*] There's this too . . .

BÉRENGER: [*excited*] Quick, show me! [*He opens the little box and takes out more documents, which he lays out on the table.*] A notebook . . . [*He turns the pages:*] 'January 13th; today I shall kill . . . January 14th, yesterday evening I pushed an old woman with gold-rimmed spectacles into the lake . . .' It's his private diary! [*He eagerly turns the pages, while* ÉDOUARD *appears very uneasy.*] 'January 23rd, nothing to kill today. January 25th, nothing to get my teeth into today either . . .'

ÉDOUARD: [*timidly*] Aren't we being indiscreet?

BÉRENGER: [*continuing*] 'January 26th, yesterday evening, just when I'd given up hope and was getting bored stiff, I managed to persuade two people to look at the Colonel's photo near the pool . . . February, tomorrow I think I'll be able to persuade a young blonde girl I've been after for some time to look at the photo . . .' Ah, that must be Dany, my poor fiancée . . .

ÉDOUARD: Seems quite likely.

BÉRENGER: [*still turning the pages*] Why look, Édouard, look, it's incredible . . .

ÉDOUARD: [*reading over* BÉRENGER'*s shoulder*] Criminology. Does that mean something?

BÉRENGER: It mean's it's an essay on crime . . . Now we've got his profession of faith, his credo . . . Here it is, you see. Have a look . . .

ÉDOUARD: [*as before: reading*] A detailed confession.

BÉRENGER: We've got him, the devil!

ÉDOUARD: [*as before: reading*] Future projects. Plan of campaign.

BÉRENGER: Dany, dear Dany, you'll be revenged. [*To ÉDOUARD:*] That's all the proof you need. We can have him arrested. Do you realize?

ÉDOUARD: [*stammering*] I didn't know . . . I didn't know . . .

BÉRENGER: So many human lives you could have saved.

ÉDOUARD: [*as before*] Yes . . . I see now. I feel awful about it. I didn't know. I never know what I've got in my briefcase, I never look inside.

BÉRENGER: Carelessness like that is unforgivable.

ÉDOUARD: It's true, forgive me, I'm so sorry.

BÉRENGER: After all, you don't mean to say these things got here all by themselves! You must have found them or been given them.

ÉDOUARD: [*coughing, mopping his brow and staggering*] I'm ashamed . . . I can't explain . . . I don't understand . . . I . . .

BÉRENGER: Don't blush. I'm really sorry for you, old chap. Don't you realize you're partly responsible for Dany's murder . . . and for so many others?

ÉDOUARD: I'm sorry . . . I didn't know.

BÉRENGER: Let's see what's to be done now. [*Heavy sigh.*] I'm afraid it's no good regretting the past. Feeling sorry won't help.

ÉDOUARD: You're right, you're right, you're right. [*Then, making an effort of memory:*] Ah yes, I remember now. It's funny, well, no, I suppose it isn't funny. The criminal sent me his private diary, his notes and index cards a very long time ago, asking me to publish them in a literary journal. That was before the murders were committed.

BÉRENGER: And yet he notes down what he's just done . . . In detail . . . It's like a log-book.

ÉDOUARD: No, no. Just then, they were only projects . . . imaginary projects. I'd forgotten the whole affair. I don't think he really intended to carry out all those crimes. His imagination carried him away. It's only later he must have thought of putting his plans into operation. *I* took them all for idle dreams of no importance . . .

BÉRENGER: [*raising his arms to Heaven*] You're so *innocent!*

ÉDOUARD: [*continuing*] Something like a murder story, poetry or literature . . .

BÉRENGER: Literature can lead anywhere. Didn't you know that?

ÉDOUARD: We can't stop writers writing, or poets dreaming.

BÉRENGER: We ought to.

ÉDOUARD: I'm sorry I didn't give it more thought and see the connection between these documents and what's been happening . . .

[*While talking,* ÉDOUARD *and* BÉRENGER *start making an attempt to collect and restore to the briefcase the various objects scattered over the table, the floor and the other pieces of furniture.*]

BÉRENGER: [*putting things back in the briefcase*] And yet the connection is simply between the intention and the act, no more no less, it's clear as daylight . . .

ÉDOUARD: [*taking a big envelope from his pocket*] There's still this!

BÉRENGER: What is it? [*They open the envelope:*] Ah, it's a map, a plan . . . Those crosses on it, what do they mean?

ÉDOUARD: I think . . . why yes . . . they're the places where the murderer's meant to be . . .

BÉRENGER: [*inspecting the map, which is spread right out on the table*] And this? Nine fifteen, thirteen twenty-seven, fifteen forty-five, nineteen three . . .

ÉDOUARD: Probably his timetable. Fixed in advance. Place by place, hour by hour, minute by minute.

BÉRENGER: . . . Twenty-three hours, nine minutes, two seconds . . .

ÉDOUARD: Second by second. He doesn't waste time. [*He says this with a mixture of admiration and indifference.*]

BÉRENGER: Let's not waste ours either. It's easy. We notify the police. Then they just have to pick him up. But we must hurry, the offices of the Prefecture close before nightfall. Then there's no one there. Between now and tomorrow he might alter his plan. Let's go quickly and see the Architect, the Superintendent.

ÉDOUARD: You're becoming quite a man of action. *I* . . .

BÉRENGER: [*continuing*] We'll show him the proof!

ÉDOUARD: [*rather weakly*] I'll come if you like.

BÉRENGER: [*excited*] Let's go, then. Not a moment to lose! We'll finish putting this all away.

[*They pile the objects as best they can into the huge briefcase, into their pockets and the lining of their hats.*]

Mustn't forget any of the documents . . . quick.

ÉDOUARD: [*still more weakly*] Yes, all right.

BÉRENGER: [*who has finished filling the briefcase, although there could still be several visiting cards and other objects on the floor and the table*] Quick, don't go to sleep, quick, quick . . . We need all the evidence . . . Now then, close it properly . . . lock it . . .

[ÉDOUARD, *who is rather harassed, tries in vain to lock the briefcase with a small key; he is interrupted by a fit of coughing.*]

Double lock it! . . . This is no time for coughing!

[ÉDOUARD *goes on trying and struggles not to cough.*]

BÉRENGER: Oh God, how clumsy you are, you've no strength in your fingers. Put some life into it, come on! . . . Get a move on. Oh, give it to me! [*He takes the brief-case and the key from* ÉDOUARD.]

ÉDOUARD: I'm sorry, I'm not very good with my hands . . .

BÉRENGER: It's *your* briefcase and you don't even know how to close it . . . Let me have the key, can't you.

[*He snatches the key quite roughly from* ÉDOUARD, *who had taken it back from him.*]

ÉDOUARD: Take it then, here you are, there.

BÉRENGER: [*fastening the briefcase*] How do you think you can close it without a key? That's it. Keep it . . .

ÉDOUARD: Thank you.

BÉRENGER: Put it in your pocket or you'll lose it.

[ÉDOUARD *obeys.*]

That's the way. Let's go . . . [*He makes for the door, reluctantly followed by* ÉDOUARD, *and turns round to say:*] Don't leave the light on, switch it off, please.

[ÉDOUARD *turns back and goes to switch off. To do this he sets the briefcase down near the chair: he will leave it behind.*]

Come on . . . Come on . . . Hurry up . . . Hurry . . . [*They both go out quickly. You can hear the door opening and slammed shut, then their footsteps in the entrance. While the noises of the town become audible again, you can see the two in the street. In their haste they bump into the* CONCIERGE, *who can be seen in front of the window.* BÉRENGER *is pulling* ÉDOUARD *along by the hand.*]

CONCIERGE: [*who has just been knocked into, while* BÉRENGER *and* ÉDOUARD *disappear*] Of all the . . . ! [*She goes on muttering, incomprehensibly.*]

CURTAIN

ACT THREE

*A wide avenue in an outlying part of the town. At the back of
the stage the view is masked by a raised pavement, a few yards
wide, with a railing along the edge. Steps, also with a railing,
leading up from street to pavement in full view of the audience.
This short flight of stone steps should be like those in some of
the old streets of Paris, such as the Rue Jean de Beauvais.
Later, at the back, there is a setting sun, large and red, but
without brilliance: the light does not come from there.
So at the back of the stage it is as though there were a kind of
wall, four and a half or six feet high, according to the height of
the stage. In the second half of the act this wall will have to
open to reveal a long street in perspective with some buildings in
the distance: the buildings of the Prefecture.
To the right of the stage, in the foreground, a small bench.
Before the curtain rises you can hear shouts of 'Long live
Mother Peep's geese! Long live Mother Peep's geese!'
The curtain goes up.
On the raised part of the stage, near the railing, is* MOTHER
PEEP, *a fat soul resembling the* CONCIERGE *of Act II. She is
addressing a crowd which is out of sight: all you can see are
two or three flags, with the device of a goose in the middle. The
white goose stands out against the green background of the
flags.*

PEEP: [*also carrying a green flag with a goose in the middle*]
People, listen to me. I'm Mother Peep and I keep the
public geese! I've a long experience of politics. Trust me
with the chariot of state, drawn by my geese, so I can

legislate. Vote for *me*. Give *me* your confidence. Me and my geese are asking for power.

[*Shouts from the crowd, the flags are waved:* 'Long live Mother Peep! Long live Mother Peep's geese!' BÉRENGER *comes in from the right, followed by* ÉDOUARD, *who is out of breath.* BÉRENGER *drags him after him, pulling him by the sleeve. In this way they cross the stage from right to left and from left to right. During the dialogue between* ÉDOUARD *and* BÉRENGER, MOTHER PEEP *cannot be heard speaking, but she will be seen gesticulating and opening her mouth wide. The acclamation of the hidden crowd forms no more than a quiet background of sound.* MOTHER PEEP'S *words and the sound of voices can of course be heard between the speeches of* ÉDOUARD *and* BÉRENGER.]

BÉRENGER: Come along, hurry up, do hurry up. Just one more effort. It's down there, right at the end. [*He points.*] Down there, the Prefecture buildings, we must arrive in time, before the offices close, in half an hour it'll be too late. The Architect, I mean the Superintendent, will have gone, and I've told you why we can't wait for tomorrow. Between now and then the killer might make off . . . or find some fresh victims! He must know I'm on his track.

ÉDOUARD: [*breathless but polite*] Wait a minute, please, you've made me run too fast.

PEEP: Fellow citizens, citizenesses . . .

BÉRENGER: Come on, come on.

ÉDOUARD: Let me have a rest . . . I can't keep going.

BÉRENGER: We haven't got time.

PEEP: Fellow citizens, citizenesses . . .

ÉDOUARD: I can't go on. [*He sits down on the bench.*]

BÉRENGER: All right, then. For one second, not more. [*He remains standing, near the bench.*] I wonder what all that crowd's for.

ÉDOUARD: Election meeting.

PEEP: Vote for us! Vote for us!

BÉRENGER: Looks like my concierge.

ÉDOUARD: You're seeing things. She's a politician, Mother Peep, a keeper of geese. A striking personality.

BÉRENGER: The name sounds familiar, but I've no time to listen.

ÉDOUARD: [*to* BÉRENGER] Sit down for a moment, you're tired.

PEEP: People, you are mystified. You shall be demystified.

BÉRENGER: [*to* ÉDOUARD] I haven't time to feel tired.

VOICE FROM THE CROWD: Down with mystification! Long live Mother Peep's geese!

ÉDOUARD: [*to* BÉRENGER] I'm sorry. Just a second. You said a second.

PEEP: I've raised a whole flock of demystifiers for you. They'll demystify you. But to demystify, you must first mystify. We need a new mystification.

BÉRENGER: We haven't time, we haven't time!

VOICE FROM THE CROWD: Up with the mystification of the demystifiers!

BÉRENGER: We haven't a moment to lose! [*He sits down all the same, consulting his watch:*] Time's getting on.

VOICE FROM THE CROWD: Up with the new mystification!

BÉRENGER: [*to* EDOUARD] Let's go.

ÉDOUARD: [*to* BÉRENGER] Don't worry. You know perfectly well the time's the same as it was just now.

PEEP: I promise you I'll change everything. And changing everything means changing nothing. You can change the names, but the things remain the same. The old mystifications haven't stood up to psychological and sociological analysis. The new one will be foolproof and cause nothing but misunderstanding. We'll bring the lie to perfection.

BÉRENGER: [*to* ÉDOUARD] Let's go!

ÉDOUARD: If you like.

BÉRENGER: [*noticing that* ÉDOUARD, *who is painfully rising to his feet, no longer has his briefcase*] Where's your briefcase?

ÉDOUARD: My briefcase? What briefcase? Ah yes, my briefcase. It must be on the bench. [*He looks on the bench.*] No. It's not on the bench.

BÉRENGER: It's extraordinary! You always have it with you!

ÉDOUARD: Perhaps it's *under* the bench.

PEEP: We're going to disalienate mankind.

BÉRENGER: [*to* ÉDOUARD] Look for it, why don't you look for it? [*They start looking for the briefcase under the bench, then on the floor of the stage.*]

PEEP: [*to crowd*] To disalienate mankind, we must alienate each individual man . . . and there'll be soup kitchens for all!

VOICE FROM THE CROWD: Soup kitchens for all and Mother Peep's geese!

BÉRENGER: [*to* ÉDOUARD] We must find it, hurry! Where could you have left it?

PEEP: [*to crowd, while* BÉRENGER *and* ÉDOUARD, *look for the briefcase, the former frantically, the latter apathetically*] We won't persecute, but we'll punish, and deal out justice. We won't colonize, we'll occupy the countries we liberate. We won't exploit men, we'll make them productive. We'll call compulsory work voluntary. War shall change its name to peace and everything will be altered, thanks to me and my geese.

BÉRENGER: [*still searching*] It's incredible, unbelievable, where can it have got to? I hope it hasn't been stolen. That would be a catastrophe, a catastrophe!

VOICE FROM THE CROWD: Long live Mother Peep's geese! Long live soup for the people!

PEEP: When tyranny is restored we'll call it discipline and liberty. The misfortune of one is the happiness of all.

BÉRENGER: [*to* ÉDOUARD] You don't realize, it's a disaster, we can't do a thing without proof, without the documents. They won't believe us.

ÉDOUARD: [*to* BÉRENGER, *nonchalantly*] Don't worry, we'll find it again. Let's look for it quietly. The great thing is to keep calm. [*They start searching again.*]

PEEP: [*to the crowd*] Our political methods will be more than scientific. They'll be para-scientific. Our reason will be founded on anger. And there'll be soup kitchens for all.

VOICE FROM THE CROWD: Long live Mother Peep! Long live the geese! Long live the geese!

VOICE FROM THE CROWD: And we'll be disalienated, thanks to Mother Peep.

PEEP: Objectivity is subjective in the para-scientific age.

BÉRENGER: [*wringing his hands, to* ÉDOUARD] It's one of the criminal's tricks.

ÉDOUARD: [*to* BÉRENGER] It's interesting, what Mother Peep says!

VOICE FROM THE CROWD: Long live Mother Peep!

BÉRENGER: [*to* ÉDOUARD] I tell you it's one of the criminal's tricks!

ÉDOUARD: [*to* BÉRENGER] You think so?

[*From the left a man appears in top hat and tails, dead drunk, holding a briefcase.*]

MAN: I am . . . [*Hiccup.*] . . . I am for . . . [*Hiccup.*] . . . the rehabilitation of the hero.

BÉRENGER: [*noticing the man*] There it is! *He's* got it! [*He makes for the* MAN.]

ÉDOUARD: Long live Mother Peep!

BÉRENGER: Where did you find that briefcase? Give it back!

MAN: Don't you favour the rehabilitation of the hero?

PEEP: [*to the crowd*] As for the intellectuals . . .

BÉRENGER: [*trying to pull the briefcase away from the* MAN] Thief! . . . Let go of that briefcase!

PEEP: [*to the crowd*] We'll make them do the goose-step! Long live the geese!

MAN: [*between two hiccups, clinging on to the briefcase*] I didn't steal it. It's *my* briefcase.

VOICE FROM THE CROWD: Long live the geese!

BÉRENGER: [*to* MAN] Where did you get it from? Where did you buy it?

MAN: [*hiccuping while being shaken by* BÉRENGER, *to* ÉDOUARD] Are you sure it's your briefcase?

ÉDOUARD: I think so . . . Looks like it.

BÉRENGER: [*to* MAN] Give it back to me, then!

MAN: I'm for the hero!

BÉRENGER: [*to* ÉDOUARD] Help me! [BÉRENGER *tackles the* MAN.]

ÉDOUARD: Yes, of course. [*He goes up to the* MAN, *but lets* BÉRENGER *tackle him on his own. He is looking at* MOTHER PEEP.]

PEEP: While they're demystifying the mystifications de-mystified long ago, the intellectuals will give us a rest and leave *our* mystifications alone.

VOICE FROM THE CROWD: Long live Mother Peep!

MAN: I tell you it's mine!

PEEP: They'll be stupid, that means intelligent. Cowardly, that means brave. Clear-sighted, that means blind.

ÉDOUARD AND VOICE FROM THE CROWD: Long live Mother Peep!

BÉRENGER: [*to* ÉDOUARD] This is not time to stand and gape. Leave Mother Peep alone.

ÉDOUARD: [*to* MAN, *coolly*] Give him the briefcase or else tell him where you bought it.

MAN: [*hiccup*] We need a hero!

BÉRENGER: [*to* MAN, *having at last managed to get hold of the briefcase*] What's inside?

MAN: I don't know. Papers.

BÉRENGER: [*opening the briefcase*] At last! Drunken sot.

ÉDOUARD: What do you mean by a hero?

PEEP: We'll march backwards and be in the forefront of history.

MAN: [*while* BÉRENGER *digs into the briefcase, and* ÉDOUARD *has a look over his shoulder, absentmindedly*] A hero? A man who dares to think against history and react against his times. [*Loudly.*] Down with Mother Peep!

BÉRENGER: [*to* MAN] You're blind drunk!

MAN: A hero fights his own age and creates a different one.

BÉRENGER: [*taking bottles of wine out of the* MAN's *briefcase*] Bottles of wine!

MAN: Half empty! That's not a crime!

PEEP: . . . for history has reason on its side . . .

MAN: [*pushed by* BÉRENGER, *he staggers and falls on his behind, exclaiming*] . . . when reason's lost its balance . . .

BÉRENGER: And are you reasonable to get drunk like this? [*To* ÉDOUARD:] Where the devil *is* your briefcase, then?

MAN: Didn't I tell you it was mine? Down with Mother Peep!

ÉDOUARD: [*still indifferent and without moving*] How do I know? You can see I'm looking for it.

VOICE FROM THE CROWD: Up Mother Peep! Up Mother Peep's geese! She changes everything by changing nothing.

BÉRENGER: [*to* ÉDOUARD] I shan't forgive you for this!

MAN: [*stumbling to his feet*] Down with Mother Peep!

ÉDOUARD: [*to* BÉRENGER, *snivelling*] Oh, don't go on at me! I'm not well.

BÉRENGER: [*to* ÉDOUARD] I can't help it, I'm sorry! Think of the state *I'm* in!

[*At this moment a little* OLD MAN, *with a pointed white beard, who looks shy and is poorly dressed, comes in from the right, holding in one hand an umbrella and in the other a huge black briefcase, identical with the one* ÉDOUARD *had in Act II.*]

MAN: [*pointing to the* OLD MAN] There's your briefcase! That must be the one!

[BÉRENGER *makes a dive at the* OLD MAN.]

PEEP: If an ideology doesn't apply to real life, we'll say it does and it'll all be perfect. The intellectuals will back us up. They'll find us anti-myths to set agains the old ones. We'll replace the myths . . .

BÉRENGER: [*to* OLD MAN] I beg your pardon, Monsieur.

PEEP: . . . by slogans . . . and the latest platitudes! . . .

OLD MAN: [*raising his hat*] I beg pardon, Monsieur, can you tell me where the Danube is?

MAN: [*to* OLD MAN] Are you for the hero?

BÉRENGER: [*to* OLD MAN] Your briefcase looks just like my friend's. [*Pointing to him:*] Monsieur Édouard.

ÉDOUARD: [*to* OLD MAN] How do you do?

VOICE FROM THE CROWD: Up Mother Peep!

OLD MAN: [*to* ÉDOUARD] Danube Street, please?

BÉRENGER: Never mind about Danube Street.

OLD MAN: Not Danube *Street*. The Danube.

MAN: But this is Paris.

OLD MAN: [*to* MAN] I know. I *am* a Parisian.

BÉRENGER: [*to* OLD MAN] It's about the briefcase!

MAN: [*to* OLD MAN] He wants to see what you've got in your briefcase.

OLD MAN: That's nobody's business. I don't even ask myself. I'm not so inquisitive.

BÉRENGER: Of your own free will or by force you're going to show us . . .

[BÉRENGER, *the* MAN *and even* ÉDOUARD *try to take the briefcase from the* OLD MAN, *who fights back, protesting.*]

OLD MAN: [*struggling*] I won't let you!

PEEP: No more profiteers. It's me and my geese . . .

[*They are all round the* OLD MAN, *harrying him and trying to take the briefcase from him: the* MAN *manages to get it away from him first, then the* OLD MAN *snatches it back and* ÉDOUARD *lays hands on it, only to lose it again to the* OLD MAN: *they also get hold of the* MAN's *briefcase again, realize their mistake when they see the bottles and give it him back, etc.*]

BÉRENGER: [*to* ÉDOUARD] Idiot!

[*He gets hold of the briefcase, the* OLD MAN *takes it back again and the* MAN *takes it from him.*]

MAN: [*offering it to* ÉDOUARD] Here it is!

[*The* OLD MAN *snatches it and tries to run away, the others catch him, etc. Meanwhile* MOTHER PEEP *is continuing her speech:*]

PEEP: . . . me and my geese who'll dole out public property. Fair shares for all. I'll keep the lion's share for myself and my geese . . .

VOICE FROM THE CROWD: Up the geese!

PEEP: . . . to give my geese more strength to draw the carts of state.

VOICE FROM THE CROWD: The lion's share for the geese! The lion's share for the geese!

MAN: [*shouting to* MOTHER PEEP] And we'll be free to criticize?

PEEP: Let's all do the goose-step!

VOICE FROM THE CROWD: The goose-step, the goose-step!

MAN: Free to criticize?

PEEP: [*turning to the* MAN] Everyone will be free to say if the goose-step's not well done!

> [*A kind of rhythmic marching is heard and the crowd shouting:* 'The goose-step, the goose-step!' *Meanwhile the* OLD MAN *has managed to escape with his briefcase. He goes off left followed by* BÉRENGER. ÉDOUARD, *who has made as if to follow* BÉRENGER *and the* OLD MAN, *turns back and goes to lie down on the bench, coughing. The* MAN *goes up to him.*]

MAN: [*to* ÉDOUARD] Aren't you well? Have a swig! [*He tries to offer him a half-empty bottle of wine.*]

ÉDOUARD: [*refusing*] No thank you.

MAN: Yes, yes. It'll do you good. Cheer you up.

ÉDOUARD: I don't want to be cheered up.

> [*The* MAN *makes the protesting* ÉDOUARD *drink; wine is spilt on the ground; the bottle too can fall and break. The* MAN *goes on making* ÉDOUARD *drink, while he speaks to* MOTHER PEEP:]

MAN: [*very drunk*] Science and art have done far more to change thinking than politics have. The real revolution is taking place in the scientists' laboratories and in the artists' stuidios. Einstein, Oppenheimer, Breton, Kandinsky, Picasso, Pavlov, they're the ones who are really responsible. They're extending our field of knowledge, renewing our vision of the world, transforming us. Soon the means of production will give everyone a chance to live. The problem of economics will settle itself. Revolutions are a barbarous weapon, myths and grudges that go off in your face. [*He takes another bottle of wine from his briefcase and has a good swig.*] Penicillin and the fight against dypsomania are worth more than politics and a change of government.

PEEP: [*to* MAN] Bastard! Drunkard! Enemy of the people! Enemy of history! [*To the crowd:*] I denounce this man: the drunkard, the enemy of history.

VOICE FROM THE CROWD: Down with history's enemy! Let's kill the enemy of history!

ÉDOUARD: [*painfully getting up*] We are all going to die. That's the only alienation that counts!

BÉRENGER: [*comes in holding the* OLD MAN'*s briefcase*] There's nothing in the briefcase.

OLD MAN: [*following* BÉRENGER] Give it back to me, give it back!

MAN: I'm a hero! I'm a hero! [*He staggers quickly to the back of the stage and climbs up the stairs to* MOTHER PEEP.] I don't think like other people! I'm going to tell them!

BÉRENGER: [*to* OLD MAN] It's not Édouard's briefcase, here it is, I'm sorry.

ÉDOUARD: Don't go. It's herosim to think against your times, but madness to say so.

BÉRENGER: It's not *your* briefcase. So where the devil *is* yours?

[*Meanwhile the* MAN *has reached the top of the steps, next to* MOTHER PEEP.]

PEEP: [*producing a huge briefcase, which has not been noticed up to now, and brandishing it*] Let's have a free discussion! [*She hits the* MAN *over the head with her briefcase.*] Rally round, my geese! Here's pasture for you!

[MOTHER PEEP *and the* MAN *fall struggling on the raised pavement. During the following scene either* MOTHER PEEP'*s head or the* MAN'*s or both at once will become visible, in the midst of a frightful hubbub of voices crying:* 'Up Mother Peep! Down with the drunk!' *Then, at the end of the following dialogue* MOTHER PEEP'*s head reappears alone, for the last time: it is hideous. Before disappearing, she says:* '*My* geese have liquidated him. But only physically.' **Punch and Judy** style.]

ÉDOUARD: The wise man says nothing. [*To* OLD MAN:] Doesn't he, Monsieur?

BÉRENGER: [*wringing his hands*] But where is it? We must have it.

OLD MAN: Where are the banks of the Danube? You can tell me *now*.

[*He straightens his clothes, shuts his briefcase and takes back his umbrella.* MOTHER PEEP'*s briefcase has opened as she hit the* MAN *and rectangular cardboard boxes have fallen from it to the ground.*]

BÉRENGER: There's your briefcase, Édouard! It's Mother Peep's. [*He notices the boxes.*] And there are the documents.

ÉDOUARD: You think so?

OLD MAN: [*to* ÉDOUARD] Damn it, he's got a mania for running after briefcases! What's he looking for?

[BÉRENGER *bends down, picks up the boxes and then comes back to the front of the stage to* ÉDOUARD *and the* OLD MAN, *looking disappointed.*]

ÉDOUARD: It's my briefcase he wants to find!

BÉRENGER: [*showing the boxes*] It's not documents! It's only the goose game!

OLD MAN: I haven't played that for a long time.

BÉRENGER: [*to* ÉDOUARD] It's no concern of yours! It's the briefcase we're after . . . the briefcase with the documents. [*To the* OLD MAN:] The evidence, to arrest the criminal!

OLD MAN: So that's it, you should have said so before.

[*It is at this moment that* MOTHER PEEP'*s head appears for the last time to make the remark already mentioned. Immediately afterwards the noise of the engine of a truck is heard, which drowns the voices of the crowd and the three characters on the stage, who go on talking and gesticulating without a word being heard. A* POLICE SERGEANT *appears, who should be unusually tall: with a white stick he taps the invisible people on the other side of the wall over the head.*]

POLICEMAN: [*only visible from head to waist, wielding the stick in one hand and blowing his whistle with the other*] Come along now, move on there. [*The crowd cries: 'The Police, the Police. Up the Police.' The* POLICEMAN *continues moving them on in the same way, so that the noise of the crowd gradually dies and fades right away. A huge military truck coming from the left blocks half the upper part of the stage.*]

ÉDOUARD: [*indifferently*] Look, an army truck!

BÉRENGER: [*to* ÉDOUARD] Never mind about that.

[*Another military truck coming from the opposite side blocks the other half of the upper part of the stage, just leaving enough room for the* POLICEMAN *in between the two trucks.*]

OLD MAN: [*to* BÉRENGER] You should have said you were looking for your friend's briefcase with the documents. I know where it is.

POLICEMAN: [*above, blowing his whistle, between the trucks*] Move along there, move along.

OLD MAN: [*to* BÉRENGER] Your friend must have left it at home, in your hurry to leave.

BÉRENGER: [*to* OLD MAN] How did you know?

ÉDOUARD: He's right, I should have thought! Were you watching us?

OLD MAN: Not at all. It's a simple deduction.

BÉRENGER: [*to* ÉDOUARD] Idiot!

ÉDOUARD: I'm sorry . . . We were in such a hurry!

[*A young* SOLDIER *gets out of the military truck, holding a bunch of red carnations. He uses it as a fan. He goes and sits on the top of the wall, the flowers in his hand, his legs dangling over the edge.*]

BÉRENGER: [*to* ÉDOUARD] Go and fetch it, go and fetch it at once! You're impossible! I'll go and warn the Superintendent, so he'll wait for us. Hurry and join me as soon as you can. The Prefecture's right at the end. In an affair like this I don't like being alone on the road. It's not pleasant. You understand?

ÉDOUARD: Of course I do, I understand. [*To* OLD MAN:] Thank you, Monsieur.

OLD MAN: [*to* BÉRENGER] Could you tell me now where the Danube Embankment is?

BÉRENGER: [*to* ÉDOUARD, *who hasn't moved*] Well, hurry up! Don't stand there! Come back quick.

ÉDOUARD: All right.

BÉRENGER: [*to* OLD MAN] I don't know, Monsieur, I'm sorry.

ÉDOUARD: [*making off very slowly to the right, where he disappears, saying nonchalantly*] All right, then, I'll hurry. I'll hurry. Won't be long. Won't be long.

BÉRENGER: [*to* OLD MAN] You must ask, ask a policeman!
[*On his way out* ÉDOUARD *nearly knocks into a* 2ND POLICEMAN, *who appears blowing his whistle and waving his white stick about too: he should be immensely tall, perhaps he could walk on stilts.*]

ÉDOUARD: [*dodging the* POLICEMAN, *who doesn't look at him*] Oh, sorry! [*He disappears.*]

BÉRENGER: [*to* OLD MAN] There's one. You can find out.

OLD MAN: He's very busy. Do you think I dare?

BÉRENGER: Yes, of course. He's all right.
[BÉRENGER *goes to the back of the stage after crying one last time after* ÉDOUARD: '*Hurry up!*' *The* OLD MAN *very shyly and hesitantly approaches the* 2ND POLICEMAN.]

OLD MAN [*timidly, to the* 2ND POLICEMAN] I beg your pardon! I beg your pardon!

BÉRENGER: [*he has gone right to the back of the stage and has one foot on the first step of the stairs*] I must hurry!

1ST POL.: [*between two blasts, pointing his white stick down at* BÉRENGER *to make him move away*] Move on, move on there.

BÉRENGER: It's terrible. What a traffic jam! I'll never, never get there. [*Addressing first one, then the other* POLICEMAN:] It's a good thing we've got you here to keep the traffic moving. You've no idea what bad luck this hold-up is for me!

OLD MAN: [*to* 2ND POLICEMAN] Excuse me, please, Monsieur, [*Before addressing the* POLICEMAN *the* OLD MAN *has respectfully removed his hat and made a low bow; the* POLICEMAN *takes no notice, he is getting excited, making signals which are answered by the* POLICEMAN *the other side of the wall with his white stick, while he too energetically blows his whistle.* BÉRENGER *goes frantically from one to the other.*]

BÉRENGER: [*to* 1ST POLICEMAN] Oh, hurry up, I've got to get by. I've a very important mission. It's humanitarian.

1ST POL.: [*who goes on blowing and signing* BÉRENGER *on with his stick*] Move along!

OLD MAN: [*to* 2ND POLICEMAN] Monsieur . . . [*To* BÉRENGER:] He won't answer. He's too busy.

BÉRENGER: Oh, these trucks are here for good. [*He looks at his watch:*] Luckily, it's still the same time. [*To* OLD MAN:] Ask him, go on and ask him, he won't bite you.

OLD MAN: [*to* 2ND POLICEMAN, *still blowing his whistle*] Please, Monsieur.

2ND POL.: [*to the* 1ST] Get them to go back! [*Sound of the engines of the still stationary trucks.*] Make them go forward! [*Same sound.*]

SOLDIER: [*to* BÉRENGER] If I knew the city I'd tell him the way. But I'm not a native.

BÉRENGER: [*to* OLD MAN] The policeman's bound to give you satisfaction. That's his privilege. Speak louder.

[*The* SOLDIER *goes on fanning himself with his bunch of red flowers.*]

OLD MAN: [*to* 2ND POLICEMAN] I'm sorry, Monsieur, listen, Monsieur.

2ND POL.: What?

OLD MAN: Monsieur, I'd like to ask you a simple question.

2ND POL.: [*sharply*] One minute! [*To* SOLDIER:] You, why have you left your truck, eh?

SOLDIER: I . . . I . . . but it's stopped!

BÉRENGER: [*aside*] Good Heavens, that Policeman's got the Superintendent's voice! Could it be him? [*He goes to have a closer look:*] No. He wasn't so tall.

2ND POL.: [*to* OLD MAN *again, while the other* POLICEMAN *is still controlling the traffic*] What's that you wanted, you there?

BÉRENGER: [*aside*] No, it's not him. His voice wasn't quite as hard as that.

OLD MAN: [*to* 2ND POLICEMAN] The Danube Embankment, please, Monsieur l'Agent, I'm sorry.

2ND POL.: [*his reply is aimed at the* OLD MAN *as well as the* 1ST POLICEMAN *and the invisible drivers of the two trucks; it precipitates a scene of general chaos, which should be comic, involving everyone; even the two trucks move*] To the left! To the right! Straight on! Straight back! Forward!

[*The* 1ST POLICEMAN, *the upper part of whom only is seen above, moves his head and white stick in obedience to his words;* BÉRENGER *makes parallel gestures, still standing on the same spot: the* SOLDIER *does the same with his bunch of flowers. The* OLD MAN *steps to the left, then to the right, then straight on, straight back and forward.*]

BÉRENGER: [*aside*] All the police have the same voice.

OLD MAN: [*returning to the* 2ND POLICEMAN] Excuse me, Monsieur, excuse me, I'm rather hard of hearing. I didn't quite understand which way you told me to go . . . for the Danube Embankment, please . . .

2ND POL.: [*to* OLD MAN] You trying to take a rise out of me? Oh no, there are *times* . . .

BÉRENGER: [*aside*] The Superintendent was much more pleasant . . .

2ND POL.: [*to* OLD MAN] Come on . . . Clear off . . . deaf or daft . . . bugger off! [*Blasts on the whistle from the* 2ND POLICEMAN, *who starts dashing about and knocks into the* OLD MAN, *who drops his walking-stick.*]

SOLDIER: [*on the steps*] Your stick, Monsieur.

OLD MAN: [*picking up his stick, to the* 2ND POLICEMAN] Don't lose your temper, Monsieur l'Agent, don't lose your temper! [*He is very frightened.*]

2ND POL.: [*still directing the traffic jam*] Left . . .

BÉRENGER: [*to* OLD MAN, *while the trucks move a little at the back of the stage, threatening for a moment to crush the* 1ST POLICEMAN] That policeman's behaviour is disgraceful!

1ST POL.: Look out, half-wits!

BÉRENGER: [*to* OLD MAN] . . . after all, he has a duty to be polite to the public.

1ST POL.: [*to the supposed drivers of the two trucks*] Left!

2ND POL.: [*as above*] Right!

BÉRENGER: [*to* OLD MAN] . . . It must be part of their regulations! . . . [*To the* SOLDIER:] Mustn't it?

1ST POL.: [*as before*] Right!

SOLDIER: [*like a child*] I don't know . . . [*Fanning himself with his flowers.*] *I've* got my flowers.

BÉRENGER: [*aside*] When I see his boss, the Architect, I'll tell him about it.

2ND POL.: [*as before*] Straight on!

OLD MAN: It doesn't matter, Monsieur l'Agent, I'm sorry
. . . [*He goes out left.*]

2ND POL.: [*as before*] To the left, left!

BÉRENGER: [*while the* 2ND POLICEMAN *is saying faster and faster
and more and more mechanically:* 'Straight on, left, right,
straight on, forwards, backwards, etc. . . .' *and the* 1ST POLICE-
MAN *repeats his orders in the same way, turning his head from
right to left, etc., like a puppet*] I think, Soldier, we're too
polite, far too nervous with the police. We've got them
into bad habits, it's our fault!

SOLDIER: [*offering the bunch of flowers to* BÉRENGER, *who has
come close to him and climbed up one or two steps*] See how
good they smell!

BÉRENGER: No thank you, I don't.

SOLDIER: Can't you see they're carnations?

BÉRENGER: Yes, but that's not the point. I've simply got to
keep going. This hold-up's a disaster!

2ND POL.: [*to* BÉRENGER, *then he goes towards the young*
SOLDIER, *when* BÉRENGER *moves away from him*] Move on.

BÉRENGER: [*moving away from the* POLICEMAN *who has just
addressed this order to him*] You don't like these trucks either,
Monsieur l'Agent. I can see that in your face. And how
right you are!

2ND POL.: [*to* 1ST POLICEMAN] Go on blowing your whistle
for a minute.

[*The* 1ST POLICEMAN *goes on as before.*]

1ST POL.: All right! Carry on!

BÉRENGER: [*to* 2ND POLICEMAN] The traffic's getting impossible. Especially when there are things . . . things that
can't wait . . .

2ND POL.: [*to the* SOLDIER, *pointing at the bunch of red carnations
the latter is still holding and fanning himself with*] Haven't you
got anything better to do than play with that?

SOLDIER: [*politely*] I'm not doing any harm, Monsieur l'Agent, that's not stopping the trucks from moving.

2ND POL.: It puts a spoke in the wheels, wise guy! [*He slaps the* SOLDIER *across the face: the* SOLDIER *says nothing. The* POLICEMAN *is so tall that he does not need to climb the steps to reach the* SOLDIER.]

BÉRENGER: [*aside, in the centre of the stage, indignantly*] Oh!

2ND POL.: [*snatching the flowers from the* SOLDIER *and hurling them into the wings*] Lunatic! Aren't you ashamed of yourself? Get back in that truck with your mates.

SOLDIER: All right, Monsieur l'Agent.

2ND POL.: [*to* SOLDIER] Look alive there, stupid bastard!

BÉRENGER: [*in the same position*] Going much too far!

SOLDIER: [*climbing back into the truck with the help of the* 1ST POLICEMAN's *fist and the* 2ND POLICEMAN's *stick*] Yes, all right, I will! [*He disappears into the truck.*]

BÉRENGER: [*in the same position*] Much too far!

2ND POL.: [*to the other invisible soldiers who are supposed to be in the trucks and who could perhaps be represented by puppets or simply be painted sitting on painted benches in the trucks*] You're blocking the road! We're fed up with your damned trucks!

BÉRENGER: [*aside, in same position*] In my view a country's done for if the police lays its hand . . . and its fingers on the Army.

2ND POL.: [*turning to* BÉRENGER] What's the matter with you? It's none of your business if . . .

BÉRENGER: But I didn't say anything, Monsieur l'Agent, not a thing . . .

2ND POL.: It's easy to guess what's going on in the minds of people of your type!

BÉRENGER: How do you know what I . . .

2ND POL.: Never you mind! You try and put your wrong thinking right.

BÉRENGER: [*stammering*] But it's not that, Monsieur, not that at all, you're mistaken, I'm sorry, I'd not . . . I'd never . . . on the contrary, I'd even . . .

2ND POL.: What are you up to here anyway? Where are your identification papers?

BÉRENGER: [*looking in his pockets*] Oh well, if that's what you want, Monsieur l'Agent . . . You've a right to see them . . .

2ND POL.: [*who is now in the centre of the stage, close to* BÉRENGER *who naturally looks very small beside him*] Come on, quicker than that. I've not time to waste!

1ST POL.: [*still above, between the two trucks*] Hey! You leaving me on my own to unscramble this traffic? [*He blows his whistle.*]

2ND POL.: [*shouting to the* 1ST] Just a minute, I'm busy. [*To* BÉRENGER:] Quicker than that. Well, aren't they coming, those papers?

BÉRENGER: [*who has found his papers*] Here they are, Monsieur l'Agent.

2ND POL.: [*examining the papers, then returning them to* BÉRENGER] Well . . . All in order!

[*The* 1ST POLICEMAN *blows his whistle and waves his white stick. The truck engines are heard.*]

1ST POL.: [*to* 2ND] Doesn't matter. We'll get him yet, next time.

BÉRENGER: [*to* 2ND POLICEMAN, *taking his papers back*] Thanks very much, Monsieur l'Agent.

2ND POL.: You're welcome . . .

BÉRENGER: [*to* 2ND POLICEMAN, *who is about to move off*] Now you know who I am and all about my case, perhaps I can ask for your help and advice.

2ND POL.: I don't know about your case.

BÉRENGER: Yes, you do, Monsieur l'Agent. You must have realized I'm looking for the killer. What else could I be doing round here?

2ND POL.: Stopping me from controlling the traffic, for example.

BÉRENGER: [*without hearing the last remark*] We can lay hands on him, I've all the evidence . . . I mean, Édouard has, he's bringing it along in his briefcase . . . Theoretically I've got it . . . meanwhile I'm off to the Prefecture, and it's still a long way . . . Can you send someone with me?

2ND POL.: Hear that? He's got a nerve!

1ST POL.: [*interrupting his mime, to the* 2ND] Is he one of us? He an informer?

2ND POL.: [*to* 1ST] He's not even that! Who does he think he is! [*He blows his whistle for the traffic.*]

BÉRENGER: Listen to me, please, this is really serious. You've seen for yourself. I'm a respectable man.

2ND POL.: [*to* BÉRENGER] What's it all got to do with you, eh?

BÉRENGER: [*drawing himself up*] I beg your pardon, but I *am* a citizen, it matters to me, it concerns us all, we're all responsible for the crimes that . . . You see, I'm a really serious citizen.

2ND POL.: [*to* 1ST] Hear that? Likes to hear himself talk.

BÉRENGER: I'm asking you once more, Monsieur l'Agent! [*To the* 1ST:] I'm asking you, too!

1ST POL.: [*still busy with the traffic*] That's enough, now.

BÉRENGER: [*continuing, to* 2ND POLICEMAN] . . . you, too: can you send someone with me to the Prefecture? I'm a friend of the Superintendent's, of the Architect's.

2ND POL.: That's not my department. I suppose even you can see I'm in 'traffic control'.

BÉRENGER: [*plucking up more courage*] I'm a friend of the Superintendent's . . .

2ND POL.: [*bending down to* BÉRENGER *and almost shouting in his ear*] I'm-in-traffic-control!

BÉRENGER: [*recoiling slightly*] Yes, I see, but . . . all the same . . . in the public interest . . . public safety, you know!

2ND POL.: Public safety? *We* look after that. When we've the time. Traffic comes first!

1ST POL.: What *is* this character? Reporter?

BÉRENGER: No, Messieurs, no, I'm *not* a reporter . . . Just a citizen, that's all . . .

1ST POL.: [*between two blasts on the whsitle*] Has he got a camera?

BÉRENGER: No, Messieurs, I haven't, search me . . . [*He turns out his pockets.*] . . . I'm *not* a reporter . . .

2ND POL.: [*to* BÉRENGER] Lucky you hadn't got it on you or I'd have smashed your face in!

BÉRENGER: I don't mind your threats. Public safety's more important than I am. He killed Dany too.

2ND POL.: Who's this Dany?

BÉRENGER: He killed her.

1ST POL.: [*between two blasts, signals and shouts of:* 'Right! Left!'] It's his tart . . .

BÉRENGER: No, Monsieur, she's my fiancée. Or was to be.

2ND POL.: [*to* 1ST] That's it all right. He wants revenge on account of his tart!

BÉRENGER: The criminal must pay for his crime!

1ST POL.: Phew! They can talk themselves silly, some of them!

2ND POL.: [*louder, turning to* BÉRENGER *again*] It's not my racket, get it? I don't give a good goddam for your story. If you're one of the boss's pals, go and see him and leave me in goddam peace.

BÉRENGER: [*trying to argue*] Monsieur l'Agent . . . I . . . I . . .

2ND POL.: [*as before, while the* 1ST POLICEMAN *laughs sardonically*]
I keep the peace, so leave *me* in peace! You know the
way . . . [*He points to the back of the stage, blocked by the trucks.*]
So bugger off, the road's clear!

BÉRENGER: Right, Monsieur l'Agent, right, Monsieur
l'Agent!

2ND POL.: [*to* 1ST, *ironically*] Let the gentleman through!
[*As though by magic the trucks move back; the whole set at the
back of the stage is movable, and so comes apart*]
Let the gentleman through!
[*The* 1ST POLICEMAN *has disappeared with the back wall and
the trucks; now, at the back of the stage, you can see a very long
street or avenue with the Prefecture buildings in the far distance
against the setting sun. A miniature tram crosses the stage far
away.*]
Let the gentleman through!

1ST POL.: [*whose face appears over the roof of one of the houses in
the street that has just appeared*] Come on, get moving! [*He
gestures to him to start moving and disappears.*]

BÉRENGER: That's just what I'm doing . . .

2ND POL.: [*to* BÉRENGER] I hate you!
[*It is the* 2ND POLICEMAN'*s turn to make a sudden dis-
appearance: the stage has got slightly darker.* BÉRENGER *is
now alone.*]

BÉRENGER: [*calling after the* 2ND POLICEMAN, *who has just disappeared*] I've more right to say that than you have! Just
now I haven't got time . . . But you haven't heard the last
of me! [*He shouts after the vanished* POLICEMAN:] You-
haven't-heard-the-last-of-me!!
[*The* ECHO *answers: last-of-me . . .
BÉRENGER *is now quite alone on the stage. The miniature
tram is no longer visible at the back. It is up to the producer,*

the designer and the electrician to bring out BÉRENGER's *utter loneliness, the emptiness around him and the deserted avenue somewhere between town and country. A part of the mobile set could disappear completely to increase the area of the stage.* BÉRENGER *should appear to be walking for a long time in the ensuing scene; if there is no revolving stage he can make the steps without advancing. It might in fact be possible to have the walls back again to give the impression of a long, narrow passage, so that* BÉRENGER *seems to be walking into some ambush; the light does not change; it is twilight, with a red sun glowing at the back of the stage. Whether the stage is broad and open or reduced by flats to represent a long, narrow street, there is a still, timeless half-light.*

While he is walking, BÉRENGER *will grow more and more anxious; at the start, he sets off, or appears to, at a fast pace; then he takes to turning round more and more frequently until his walk has become hesitant; he looks to right and left, and then behind him again, so that in the end he appears to be on the point of flight, ready to turn back; but he controls himself with difficulty and after a great effort decides to go forawrd again; if the set is movable and can be changed without having to lower the curtain or the lights,* BÉRENGER *might just as well walk from one end of the stage to the other, and then come back, etc.*

*Finally, he will advance cautiously, glancing all round him; and yet, at the end of the Act when the last character in the play makes his appearance—or is first heard, or heard and seen at the same time—*BÉRENGER *will be taken by surprise: so this character should appear just when* BÉRENGER *is looking the other way. The appearance of this character must, however, be prepared for by* BÉRENGER *himself:* BÉRENGER's *mounting anguish should make the audience aware that the character is getting nearer and nearer.*]

BÉRENGER: [*starting to walk, or appearing to, and at the same time turning his head in the direction of the* POLICEMEN *towards the wings on the right, and shaking his fist at them*] I can't do everything at once. Now for the murderer. It'll be your turn next. [*He walks in silence for a second or two, stepping it out.*] Outrageous attitude! I don't believe in reporting people, but I'll talk to the Chief Superintendent about it, you bet I will! [*He walks in silence.*] I hope I'm not too late! [*The noise of the wind: a dead leaf flutters down and* BÉRENGER *turns up his overcoat collar.*] And now, on top of everything else, the wind's got up. And the light's going. Will Édouard be able to catch me up in time? Will he catch me up in time? He's so slow! [*He walks on in silence the set changes.*] Everything will have to be changed. First we must start by reforming the police force . . . All they're good for is teaching you manners, but when you really *need* them . . . when you want them to protect you . . . they couldn't care less . . . they let you down . . . [*He looks round:*] They and their trucks, they're a long way off already . . . Better hurry. [*He sets off again.*] I *must* get there before it's dark. It can't be too safe on the road. Still a long way . . . Not getting any nearer . . . I'm not making any progress. It's as though I wasn't moving at all. [*Silence.*] There's no end to this avenue and its tramlines. [*Silence.*] . . . There's the boundary anyway, the start of the Outer Boulevards . . . [*He walks in silence.*] I'm shivering. Because of the cold wind. You'd think I was frightened, but I'm not. I'm used to being alone . . . [*He walks in silence.*] I've always been alone . . . And yet I love the human race, but at a distance. What's that matter, when I'm interested in the fate of mankind? Fact is, I *am doing* something . . . [*He smiles.*] Doing . . . acting . . . acting, not play-acting, doing! Well, really I'm even running risks,

you might say, for mankind . . . and for Dany too. Risks?
The Civil Service will protect me. Dear Dany, those policemen defiled your memory. I'll make them pay. [*He looks
behind him, ahead, then behind again; he stops.*] I'm half way
there. Not quite. Nearly . . . [*He sets off again at a not very
determined pace; while he walks he glances behind him:*]
Édouard! That you, Édouard? [*The Echo answers: ouard
. . . ouard . . .*] No . . . it's not Édouard . . . Once he's
arrested, bound hand and foot, out of harm's way, the
spring will come back for ever, and every city will be
radiant . . . I shall have my reward. That's not what I'm
after. To have done my duty, that's enough . . . So long
as it's not too late, so long as it's not too late. [*Sound of the
wind or the cry of an animal.* BÉRENGER *stops.*] Supposing I
went back . . . to look for Édouard? We could go to the
Prefecture tomorrow. Yes, I'll go tomorrow, with
Édouard . . . [*He turns in his tracks and takes a step on the road
back.*] No. Édouard's sure to catch me up in a moment or
two. [*To himself:*] Think of Dany. I must have revenge for
Dany. I must stop the rot. Yes, yes, I know I can. Besides,
I've gone too far now, it's darker that way than the way
I'm going. The road to the Prefecture is still the safest.
[*He shouts again:*] Édouard! Édouard!

ECHO: É-dou-ard . . . ou . . . ard . . .

BÉRENGER: Can't see now whether he's coming or not. Perhaps he's quite near. Go on again. [*Setting off again with
great caution.*] Doesn't seem like it, but I've covered some
ground . . . Oh yes I have, no doubt about it . . . You
wouldn't think so, but I *am* advancing . . . advancing
. . . Ploughed fields on my right, and this deserted
street . . . No risk of a traffic jam now anyway, you can
keep going. [*He laughs. The echo vaguely repeats the laugh.*
BÉRENGER, *scared, looks round:*] What's that? . . . It's the

echo . . . [*He resumes his walking.*] No one there, stupid . . .
Over there, who's that? There, behind that tree! [*He
rushes behind a leafless tree, which could be part of the moving
scene.*] Why, no, it's nobody . . . [*The leaf of an old newspaper falls from the tree.*] Aah! . . . Afraid of a newspaper
now. What a fool I am! [*He bursts out laughing. The echo
repeats: . . . fool . . . I . . . am . . . and distorts the laugh.*] I
must get further . . . I must go on! Advancing under cover
of the Civil Service . . . advancing . . . I must . . . I must
. . . [*Halt.*] No, no. It's not worth it, in any case I'll arrive
too late. Not my fault, it's the fault of the . . . the fault of
the . . . of the traffic, the hold-up made me late . . . And
above all it's Édouard's fault . . . he forgets everything,
every blessed thing . . . Perhaps the murderer will strike
again tonight . . . [*With a start:*] I've simply got to stop
him. I *must* go. I'm going. [*Another two or three paces in the
direction of the supposed Prefecture:*] Come to think of it, it's
all the same really, as it's too late. Another victim here or
there, what's it matter in the state we're in . . . We'll go
tomorrow, go tomorrow, Édouard and I, and much
simpler that way, the offices will be closed this evening,
perhaps they are already . . . What good would it do to
. . . [*He shouts off right into the wings:*] Édouard! Édouard!
Echo: E . . . ard . . . e . . . ard . . .

Bérenger: He won't come now. No point in thinking he
will. It's too late. [*He looks at his watch:*] My watch has
stopped . . . Never mind, there's no harm putting it off . . .
I'll go tomorrow, with Édouard! . . . The Superintendent
will arrest him tomorrow. [*He turns round.*] Where am I? I
hope I can find my way home? It's in this direction! [*He
turns round again quickly and suddenly sees the* Killer *quite
close to him.*] Ah! . . .

[*The set has of course stopped changing. In fact there is*
165

practically no scenery. All there is is a wall and a bench. The empty waste of a plain and a slight glow on the horizon. The two characters are picked out in a pale light, while the rest is in semi-darkness. Derisive laugh from the KILLER *: he is very small and puny, ill-shaven, with a torn hat on his head and a shabby old gaberdine; he has only one eye, which shines with a steely glitter, and a set expression on his still face; his toes are peeping out of the holes in his old shoes. When the* KILLER *appears, laughing derisively, he should be standing on the bench or perhaps somewhere on the wall: he calmly jumps down and approaches* BÉRENGER, *chuckling unpleasantly, and it is at this moment that one notices how small he is. Or possibly there is no* KILLER *at all.* BÉRENGER *could be talking to himself, alone in the half-light.*]

It's him, it's the killer! [*To the* KILLER:] So it's you, then! [*The* KILLER *chuckles softly:* BÉRENGER *glances round, anxiously.*]

Nothing but the dark plain all around . . . You needn't tell me, I can see that as well as you.

[*He looks towards the distant Prefecture. Soft chuckle from the* KILLER.]

The Prefecture's too far away? That's what you just meant? I know.

[*Chuckle from the* KILLER.]

Or was that me talking?

[*Chuckle from the* KILLER.]

You're laughing at me! I'll call the police and have you arrested.

[*Chuckle from the* KILLER.]

It's no good, you mean, they wouldn't hear me?

[*The* KILLER *gets down from the bench or the wall and approaches* BÉRENGER, *horribly detached and vaguely chuckling, both hands in his pockets. Aside:*]

166

Those dirty cops left me alone with him on purpose. They wanted to make me believe it was just a private feud. [*To the* KILLER, *almost shouting:*] Why? Just tell me why?

[*The* KILLER *chuckles and gives a slight shrug of the shoulders: he is quite close to* BÉRENGER, *who should appear not only bigger but also stronger than the almost dwarf-like* KILLER. BÉRENGER *has a burst of nervous laughter.*]

Oh, you really are rather puny, aren't you? Too puny to be a criminal! I'm not afraid of you! Look at me, look how much stronger I am. I could knock you down, knock you flying with a flick of my fingers. I could put you in my pocket. Do you realize?

[*Same chuckle from the* KILLER.]

I'm-not-afraid-of-you!

[*Chuckle from the* KILLER.]

I could squash you like a worm. But I won't. I want to understand. You're going to answer my questions. After all, you are a human being. You've got reasons, perhaps. You must explain, or else I don't know what . . . You're going to tell me why . . . Answer me!

[*The* KILLER *chuckles and gives a slight shrug of the shoulders.* BÉRENGER *should be pathetic and naïve, rather ridiculous; his behaviour should seem sincere and grotesque at the same time, both pathetic and absurd. He speaks with an eloquence that should underline the tragically worthless and outdated commonplaces he is advancing.*]

Anyone who does what you do does it perhaps because . . . Listen . . . You've stopped me from being happy, and stopped a great many more . . . In that shining district of the town, which would surely have cast its radiance over the whole world . . . a new light radiating from France! If you've any feeling left for you country . . . it would have shone on you, would have moved you too, as well as

countless others, would have made you happy in yourself
. . . a question of waiting, it was only a matter of patience
. . . *im*patience, that's what spoils everything. . . yes, you
would have been happy, happiness would have come
even to you, and it would have spread, perhaps you didn't
know, perhaps you didn't believe it . . . You were wrong
. . . Well, it's your own happiness you've destroyed as
well as mine and that of all the others . . .

[*Slight chuckle from the* KILLER.]

I suppose you don't believe in happiness. You think
happiness is impossible in this world? You want to destroy
the world because you think it's doomed. Don't you?
That's it, isn't it? Answer me!

[*Chuckle from the* KILLER.]

I suppose you never thought for a single moment that
you'd got it wrong. You were sure you were right. It's just
your stupid pride. Before you finally make up your mind
about this, at least let other people experiment for themselves. They're trying to realize a practical and technical
ideal of happiness, here and now, on this earth of ours;
and they'll succeed, perhaps, how can *you* tell? If they
don't, then you can think again . . .

[*Chuckle from the* KILLER.]

You're a pessimist?

[*Chuckle from the* KILLER.]

You're a nihilist?

[*Chuckle from the* KILLER.]

An anarchist?

[*Chuckle from the* KILLER.]

Perhaps you don't like happiness? Perhaps happiness is
different for you? Tell me your ideas about life. What's
your philosophy? Your motives? Your aims? Answer me!

[*Chuckle from the* KILLER.]

Listen to me: you've hurt me personally in the worst possible way, destroying everything . . . all right, forget that . . . I'll not talk about myself. But you killed Dany! What had Dany done to you? She was a wonderful creature, with a few faults of course, I suppose she was rather hot-tempered, liked her own way, but she had a kind heart, and beauty like that is an excuse for anything! If you killed every girl who liked her own way just because she liked her own way, or the neighbours because they make a noise and keep you awake, or someone for holding different opinions from you, it would be ridiculous, wouldn't it? Yet that's what you do! Don't you? Don't you?

[*Chuckle from the* KILLER.]

We won't talk about Dany any more. She was my fiancée, and you might believe it's all just a personal matter. But tell me this . . . what had that Officer in the Engineers done to you, that Staff Officer?

[*Chuckle from the* KILLER.]

All right, I know . . . I understand, there are some people who hate a uniform. Rightly or wrongly they see it as the symbol of an abuse of power, of tyranny, and of war, which destroys civilizations. Right: we won't raise the question, it might take us too far, from that woman . . .

[*Chuckle from the* KILLER.]

. . . you know the one I mean, that young redhead, what had *she* done to you? What had you got against *her*? Answer me!

[*Chuckle from the* KILLER.]

We'll suppose you hate women, then: perhaps they betrayed you, didn't love you, because you're not, let's face it, you're not much to look at . . . it's not fair, I agree, but there's more than just the sexual side to life, there are

some religious people who've given up that for all time
. . . you can find satisfaction of a different kind in life and
overcome that feeling of resentment . . .

[*Chuckle from the* KILLER.]

But the child, that child, what had he done to you? Children can't be guilty of anything, can they? You know the one I mean: the little fellow you pushed into the pool with the woman and the officer, poor little chap . . . our hopes are in the children, no one should touch a child; everyone agrees about that.

[*Chuckle from the* KILLER.]

Perhaps you think the human race is rotten in itself. Answer me!! You want to punish the human race even in a child, the least impure of all . . . We could debate the problem, if you like publicly, defend and oppose the motion, what do you say?

[*Chuckle from the* KILLER, *who shrugs his shoulders.*]

Perhaps you kill all these people out of kindness! To save them from suffering! For you, life is just suffering! Perhaps you want to cure people of the haunting fear of death? You think like others before you, that man is and always will be the sick animal, in spite of all social, technical or scientific progress, and I suppose you want to carry out a sort of universal mercy-killing? Well, you're mistaken, you're wrong. Answer me!

[*Chuckle from the* KILLER.]

Anyway, if life's of little value, if it's too short, the suffering of mankind will be short too: whether men suffer thirty or forty years, ten years more or less, what's it matter to you? Let people suffer if that's what they want. Let them suffer as long as they're willing to suffer . . . Besides, time goes by, a few years hardly count, they'll have a whole eternity of *not* suffering. Let them die in their own time and it will all be over quite soon. Everything will flicker out and finish on its own. Don't hurry things up, there's no point. *Sympathy (persuasion.*

[*Chuckle from the* KILLER.] → *Bérenger is a twit / that mismakes you sorry for him*

Why, you're putting yourself in an absurd position, if you think you're doing mankind a service by destroying it, you're wrong, that's stupid! Aren't you afraid of ridicule? Eh? Answer me that!

[*Chuckle from the* KILLER: *loud, nervous laugh from* BÉRENGER. *Then, after watching the* KILLER *for a while:*]

I see this doesn't interest you. I haven't laid my finger on the real problem, on the spot that really hurts. Tell me: do you hate mankind? Do you hate mankind?

[*Chuckle from the* KILLER.]

But why? Answer me!

[*Chuckle from the* KILLER.]

If that *is* the case, don't vent your spleen on men, that's no good, it only makes you suffer yourself, it hurts to hate, better despise them, yes, I'll allow you to despise them, isolate yourself from them, go and live in the mountains, become a shepherd, why not, and you'll live among the sheep and dogs.

[*Chuckle from the* KILLER.]

You don't like animals either? You don't love anything that's alive? Not even the plants? . . . What about stones and stars, the sun and the blue sky?

[*Chuckle and shrug of the shoulders from the* KILLER.]

No. No, I'm being silly. One can't hate everything. Do you believe society's rotten, that it can't be improved, that revolutionaries are fools? Or do you believe the existence of the universe is a mistake?

[*The* KILLER *shrugs his shoulders.*]

Why can't you answer me, answer me! Oh! Argument's

impossible with you! Listen, you'll make me angry, I warn you! No . . . no . . . I mustn't lose my self-control. I *must* understand you. Don't look at me like that with your glittering eye. I'm going to talk frankly. Just now I meant to have my revenge, for myself and the others. I wanted to have you arrested, sent to the guillotine. Vengeance is stupid. Punishment's not the answer. I was furious with you. I was after your blood . . . as soon as I saw you . . . not *immediately*, not that very moment, no, but a few seconds later, I . . . it sounds silly, you won't believe me, and yet I must tell you . . . yes . . . you're a human being, we're the same species, we've got to understand each other, it's our duty, a few seconds later, I loved you, or almost . . . because we're brothers, and if I hate *you*, I can't help hating *myself*. . . .

[*Chuckle from the* KILLER.]

Don't laugh: it exists, fellow feeling, the brotherhood of man, I know it does, don't sneer . . .

[*Chuckle and shrug of the shoulders from the* KILLER.]

. . . ah . . . but you're a . . . you're nothing but a . . . now listen to this. *We*'re the strongest, *I*'m stronger physically than you are, you're a helpless feeble little runt! What's more, I've the law on my side . . . the police!

[*Chuckle from the* KILLER.]

Justice, the whole force of law and order!

[*Chuckle from the* KILLER.]

I mustn't, I *mustn't* get carried away . . . I'm sorry . . .

[*Chuckle from the* KILLER: BÉRENGER *mops his brow*.]

You've got more self-control than I have . . . but I'll calm down, I'll calm down . . . no need to be afraid . . . You don't *seem* very frightened . . . I mean, don't hold it against me . . . but you're not even scared, are you? . . . No, it's not that, that's not what I mean . . . Ah yes, yes . . . perhaps you don't realize. [*Very loud.*] Christ died on the Cross for *you*, it was for *you* he suffered, he *loves* you . . . And you really need to be loved, though you think you don't!

[*Chuckle from the* KILLER.]

I swear to you that the blessed saints are pouring out tears for you, torrents and oceans of tears. You're soaked in their tears from head to foot, it's impossible for you not to feel a little wet!

[*Chuckle from the* KILLER.]

Stop sneering like that. You don't believe me, you don't believe me! . . . If Christ's not enough for you, I give you my solemn word I'll have an army of saviours climbing new Calvaries, just for you, and have them crucified for love of you! . . . They must exist and I'll find them! Will that do?

[*Chuckle from the* KILLER.]

Do you want the whole world to destroy itself to give you a moment of happiness, to make you smile just once? That's possible too! I'm ready myself to embrace you, to be one of your comforters; I'll dress your wounds, because you *are* wounded, aren't you? You've suffered, haven't you? You're still suffering? I'll take pity on you, you know that now. Would you like me to wash your feet? Then perhaps you'd like some new shoes? You loathe sloppy sentimentality. Yes, I can see it's no good trying to touch your feelings. You don't want to be trapped by tenderness! You're afraid it'll make a fool of you. You've a temperament that's diametrically opposed to mine. All men are brothers, of course, they're like each other, but they're not always alike. And they've one thing in common. There must be one thing in common, a common language . . . What is it? What is it?

[*Chuckle from the* KILLER.]

Ah, I know now, I know . . . You see, I'm right not to give up hope for you. We can speak the language of reason. It's the language that suits you best. You're a scientific man, aren't you, a man of the modern era, I've guessed it now, haven't I, a cerebral man? You deny love, you doubt charity, it doesn't enter into your calculations, and you think charity's a cheat, don't you, don't you?

[*Chuckle from the* KILLER.]

I'm not blaming you. I don't despise you for that. After all, it's a point of view, a possible point of view, but between ourselves, listen here: what do you get out of all this? What good does it do *you*? Kill people if you like, but in your mind . . . leave them alive in the flesh.

[*Shrug of the shoulders and chuckle from the* KILLER.]

Oh, yes, in your opinion that would be a comic contradiction. Idealism you'd call it, you're for a practical philosophy, you're a man of action. Why not? But where's the action leading you? What's the final object? Have you asked yourself the question of ultimate ends?

[*A more accentuated chuckle and shrug of the shoulders from the* KILLER.]

It's an action that's utterly sterile in fact, it wears you out. It only brings trouble . . . Even if the police shut their eyes to it, which is what usually happens, what's the good of all the effort, the fatigue, the complicated preparations and exhausting nights on the watch . . . people's contempt for you? Perhaps you don't mind. You earn their fear, it's true, that's something. All right, but what do you do with it? It's not a form of capital. You don't even exploit it. Answer me!

[*Chuckle from the* KILLER.]

You're poor now, aren't you? Do you want some money?
I can find you work, a decent job . . . No. You're not poor?
Rich then? . . . Aaah, I see, neither rich nor poor!

[*Chuckle from the* KILLER.]

I see, you don't want to work: well, you shan't then. I'll
look after you, or as I'm poor myself, I'd better say I'll
arrange for me and my friends to club together, I'll talk
to the Architect about it. And you'll lead a quiet life.
We'll go to the cafés and the bars, and I'll introduce you
to girls who aren't too difficult . . . Crime doesn't pay. So
stop being a criminal and we'll pay you. It's only common
sense.

[*Chuckle from the* KILLER.]

You agree? Answer, answer, can't you? You understand
the language! . . . Listen I'm going to make you a painful
confession. Often, I have my doubts about everything too.
But don't tell anyone. I doubt the point of living, the
meaning of life, doubt my own values and every kind of
rational argument. I no longer know what to hang on to,
perhaps there's no more truth or charity. But if that's the
case, be philosophical; if all is vanity, if charity is vanity,
crime's just vanity too . . . When you know everything's
dust and ashes, you'd be a fool if you set any store by
crime, for that would be setting store by life . . . That
would mean you were taking things seriously . . . and then
you'd be in complete contradiction with yourself. [*Gives
nervous laugh.*] Eh? It's obvious. It's only logic, I caught
you there. And then you'd be in a bad way, you'd be
feeble minded, a poor specimen. Logically we'd have the
right to make fun of you! Do you want us to make fun of
you? Of course you don't. You must have your pride,
respect your own intelligence. There's nothing worse than
being stupid. It's much more compromising than being a

criminal, even madness has a halo round it. But to be stupid? To be ignorant? Who can accept that?

[*Chuckle from the* KILLER.]

Everyone will point at you and laugh!

[*Chuckle from the* KILLER. BÉRENGER *is obviously more and more baffled.*]

There's the idiot going by, there's the idiot! Ha! Ha! Ha!

[*Chuckle from the* KILLER.]

He kills people, gives himself all that trouble—Ha! Ha! Ha!—and doesn't get anything out of it, it's all for nothing ... Ha! Ha! Do you want to hear that said, be taken for an idiot, an idealist, a crank who 'believes' in something, who 'believes' in crime, the simpleton! Ha! Ha! Ha!

[*Chuckle from the* KILLER.]

... Who believes in crime for its own sake! Ha! Ha! [*His laugh suddenly freezes.*] Answer me! That's what they'll say, yes ... if there's anyone left to say it ... [*Wrings his hands, clasps them, kneels down and begs the* KILLER:] I don't know what else I can say to you. We must have done something to hurt you.

[*Chuckle from the* KILLER.]

Perhaps there's no wrong on our side.

[*Chuckle from the* KILLER.]

I don't know. It may be my fault, it may be yours. It may not be yours or mine. It may not be anyone's fault. What you're doing may be wrong or it may be right, or it may be neither right nor wrong. I don't know how to tell. It's possible that the survival of the human species is of no importance, so what does it matter if it disappears ... perhaps the whole universe is no good and you're right to want to blast it all, or at least nibble at it, creature by creature, piece by piece ... or perhaps that's wrong. I don't know any more, I just don't know. You may be mistaken, perhaps mistakes don't really exist, perhaps it's we who are mistaken to want to exist . . . say what you believe, can't you? *I* can't. *I* can't.

[*Chuckle from the* KILLER.]

Some think just *being* is a mistake, an aberration.

[*Chuckle from the* KILLER.]

Perhaps your pretended motives are only a mask for the real cause you unconsciously hide from yourself. Who knows. Let's sweep all these reasons away and forget the trouble you've already caused . . .

[*Chuckle from the* KILLER.]

Agreed? You kill without reason in that case, and I beg you, without reason I implore you, yes, please *stop* . . . There's no reason why you should, naturally, but please stop, just because there's *no reason* to kill or not to kill. You're killing people for nothing, save them for nothing. Leave people alone to live their stupid lives, leave them all alone, even the policemen . . . Promise, me you'll stop for at least a month . . . *please* do as I ask, for a week, for forty-eight hours, to give us a chance to breathe . . . You will do that, won't you? . . .

[*The* KILLER *chuckles softly; very slowly he takes from his pocket a knife with a large shining blade and plays with it.*]

You filthy dirty moronic imbecile! You're ugly as a monkey! Fierce as a tiger, stupid as a mule . . .

[*Slight chuckle from the* KILLER.]

I'm on my knees, yes . . . but it's not to beg for mercy . . .

[*Slight chuckle from the* KILLER.]

It's to take better aim . . . I'm going to finish you, and then I'll stamp on you and squash you to pulp, you stinking rotten carcass of a hyena! [*Takes two pistols from his pockets and aims them at the* KILLER, *who doesn't move a muscle.*] I'll kill you, you're going to pay for it, I'll shoot and shoot, and then I'll hang you, I'll chop you into a thousand pieces, I'll throw your ashes into Hell with the excrement you came from, you vomit of Satan's mangy cur, criminal cretin . . .

[*The* KILLER *goes on playing with the blade of his knife; slight chuckle and shrug of the shoulders, but he does not move.*] Don't look at me like that, I'm not afraid of you, you shame creation.

[BÉRENGER *aims without firing at the* KILLER, *who is two paces away, standing still, chuckling unpleasantly and quietly raising his knife.*]

Oh . . . how weak my strength is against your cold determination, your ruthlessness! And what good are bullets even, against the resistance of an infinitely stubborn will! [*With a start:*] But I'll get you, I'll get you . . .

[*Then, still in front of the* KILLER, *whose knife is raised and who is chuckling and quite motionless,* BÉRENGER *slowly lowers his two old-fashioned pistols, lays them on the ground, bends his head and then, on his knees with his head down and his arms hanging at his side, he stammers:*]

Oh God! There's nothing we can do. What can we do . . . What can we do . . .

[*While the* KILLER *draws nearer, still chuckling, but very, very softly.*]

CURTAIN

London, August 1957

MAID TO MARRY

MAID TO MARRY

First produced in Paris by Jacques Polieri at the Théâtre de la Huchette, the 1st September, 1953.

CHARACTERS:
    THE GENTLEMAN
    THE LADY
    THE GENTLEMAID
    The LADY *is wearing a flowered hat with a big hatpin, a long dress and a short tight-fitting purple jacket. She is carrying a handbag. The* GENTLEMAN *has a frock-coat, a high stiff collar and stiff cuffs, a black cravat and a white beard.*
    They are sitting on a bench in a public park.

LADY: My daughter, let me tell you, was quite brilliant in her studies.

GENTLEMAN: I didn't know, but I'm not surprised. I knew she had plenty of pluck.

LADY: *I've* had no cause to complain, like so many parents. She's always given us perfect satisfaction.

GENTLEMAN: The credit is all yours. You brought her up properly. The model child is very rare, especially nowadays.

LADY: How right you are! . . .

GENTLEMAN: In my time children were far more obedient, more attached to their parents. They understood the sacrifices they make, their material problems and their difficulties . . . though from some points of view it's better for them not to.

LADY: I agree! . . . They were also far more . . .

GENTLEMAN: They were far more numerous.

LADY: Indeed they were. It seems the birth-rate's falling in France.

GENTLEMAN: It has its ups and downs. Just now it rather shows a tendency to rise again. But we can hardly make up for the lean years! . . .

LADY: I should say not indeed, you're certainly right there! Just imagine!

GENTLEMAN: What can you expect? It's not easy to bring children up at the present time! . . .

LADY: Indeed it's not! You don't have to tell *me* that! It's costing more and more to keep alive! And think of all the things they need! What is there they *don't* want?

GENTLEMAN: What's it all leading to? . . . Today human life is the only thing that's cheap!

LADY: Oh . . . I *do* so agree with that! . . . Now that's *very* true . . . You're *perfectly* right there . . .

GENTLEMAN: There are earthquakes, accidents, cars and all sorts of other vehicles like aeroplanes, social sickness, voluntary suicide, the atom bomb . . .

LADY: Oh, *that thing*! . . . It appears it's changed the weather for us! We don't know where we are with our seasons now, it's upset everything! . . . And if only that was all . . . but look, listen, do you know what I've heard people say? . . .

GENTLEMAN: Oh! . . . They say so many things! If you had to believe everything you hear!

LADY: That's true of course . . . There'd be no end to it, indeed there wouldn't! . . . The papers too, there's a pack of lies for you, lies, all lies! . . .

GENTLEMAN: Do as I do, Madame, trust nobody, believe in nothing, don't let them stuff your brain with rubbish! . . .

LADY: I agree. You're better off without. Indeed you are. You've got *your* head screwed on all right. You really have.

GENTLEMAN: Oh, I just *use* mine, that's all!

LADY: You're right there! . . . But you can't say the same of everyone . . .

GENTLEMAN: Nowadays you see, Madame, with all our amusements, entertainment and excitement, the cinema, income tax, gramophone record libraries, telephone, radio, air travel, big department stores . . .

LADY: Ah yes, now you've *said* it!

GENTLEMAN: The prisons, the Grand Boulevards, Social Security, and all that . . .

LADY: How right you are . . .

GENTLEMAN: All these things that make the charm of modern life have changed men and women, changed them to such a point that they're unrecognizable! . . .

LADY: Not changed them for the better either, *now* you've said it.

GENTLEMAN: And yet we can't deny progress, when we see it progressing every day . . .

LADY: How right you are . . .

GENTLEMAN: . . . in technology, applied science, mechanics, literature and art . . .

LADY: Of course. We must be fair. It isn't nice to be *un*fair.

GENTLEMAN: You could even go so far as to say that civilization's constantly developing, and in the right direction, thanks to the united efforts of all the nations . . .

LADY: Perfectly true. I was just about to say the same thing.

GENTLEMAN: We've come a long way since the days of our ancestors, who used to live in caves and gobble each other up and feed on sheepskins! . . . What a long way we've come!

LADY: Yes, we have, haven't we? . . . And central heating, Monsieur, what about central heating? Did they have that in their caves?

GENTLEMAN: Well now, dear lady, when I was a small child . . .

LADY: Such a pretty age!

GENTLEMAN: . . . I used to live in the country. I remember it was still the sun that kept us warm, winter and summer alike. We used to light our homes with oil—it's true it wasn't so dear in those days—and sometimes even with candles! . . .

LADY: That happens even today, when the electricity fails.

GENTLEMAN: Machines are not perfect either. They were invented by man and they've all *his* faults!

LADY: Don't talk to me about the faults of men. Oh lala! I know all about that, they're no better than the women, they're all alike, nothing to choose between them.

GENTLEMAN: Of course. So why expect a man to do a job even a machine can't do . . .

LADY: I admit I'd never thought of that . . . yes, when you really come to think about it, it's possible after all, why not? . . .

GENTLEMEN: You see, Madame, mankind's future's in the future. It's just the opposite for animals and plants . . . But we mustn't think of the machine as a *Deus ex machina* who'll take the place of God and progress without the slightest effort on our part. On the contrary, Madame . . .

LADY: I never said we should!

GENTLEMEN: On the contrary, I say, man is still the best human machine! It's man who controls the machine . . . because he's the mind.

LADY: Now *you've* said it.

GENTLEMAN: ... and a machine's just a machine, except for the calculating machine, which calculates by itself ...

LADY: That's very true, it calculates by itself, what you say is perfectly correct ...

GENTLEMAN: It's just the exception that proves the rule ... Look here, just now we were talking about oil and candles. In those days an egg cost a sou and not a sou more! ...

LADY: Impossible!

GENTLEMAN: Believe it or not! ...

LADY: It's not that I doubt your word!

GENTLEMAN: You could dine for twenty sous, food cost nothing then ...

LADY: It's a different story now!

GENTLEMAN: ... You could have a pair of good shoes, good leather too, for three francs seventy-five centimes ... Young folk today don't know what that means!

LADY: They don't know when they're well-off! The young are so ungrateful!

GENTLEMAN: Nowadays everything's a thousand times dearer. So how can we really maintain that the machine's a happy invention and progress a good thing?

LADY: We can't, of course!

GENTLEMAN: You'll probably say that progress can be good or bad, like Jews or Germans or films! ...

LADY: Oh no, I wouldn't say a thing like that!

GENTLEMAN: Why not? You could if you liked, you've a right to, haven't you?

LADY: Of course I have! ...

GENTLEMAN: I respect everyone's right to an opinion. My ideas are up-to-date. After all there has been a French Revolution, and the Crusades, and the Inquisition, and Kaiser William, the Popes, the Renaissance, Louis XIV and all that trouble for nothing! . . . We've paid dearly for the right to say whatever comes into our heads, without having people make fun of us . . .

LADY: We certainly have! . . . This land's our home! . . . We won't have anyone come and upset us in our own place . . .

GENTLEMAN: And Joan of Arc? Have you ever wondered what *she* would say, if she could see all this?

LADY: That's a question I've asked myself more than once!

GENTLEMAN: Radio! . . . And *she* used to live in an old cottage! With all these modern transformations, she wouldn't know it any more!

LADY: Oh no, she certainly wouldn't know it if she saw it now!

GENTLEMAN: And yet, perhaps she would after all!

LADY: Yes, you're right, perhaps she would after all!

GENTLEMAN: To think she was burnt alive by those Englishmen and then they became our allies . . .

LADY: Who'd ever have thought it?

GENTLEMAN: There are *some* good Englishmen too . . .

LADY: But they're mostly bad!

GENTLEMAN: You needn't think the Corsicans are any better!

LADY: That's not what I meant! . . .

GENTLEMAN: At least they serve one good purpose. All French postmen are Corsican. Who'd bring us our mail if there weren't any postmen!

LADY: They're a necessary evil.

GENTLEMAN: Evil is never necessary.

LADY: How right you are, that's very true!

GENTLEMAN: Don't think I look down on a postman's profession.

LADY: Every profession has its points.

GENTLEMAN: [*rising to his feet*] Madame, that is a profound observation! It deserves to pass into the language as a proverb. Allow me to congratulate you . . . [*He kisses her hand.*] Here is the *Croix d'honneur*. [*He pins a medal on the* LADY's *bosom.*]

LADY: [*embarrassed*] Oh, Monsieur! . . . After all, I'm only a woman! . . . But if you really mean it!

GENTLEMAN: I promise you I do, Madame. The Truth may spring from any brain . . .

LADY: Flatterer!

GENTLEMAN: [*sitting down again*] Madame, you've laid your finger on the principal vice of our society, which I detest and condemn in its entirety, without wishing to cut myself off from it . . .

LADY: You must never do that.

GENTLEMAN: Our society, Madame, no longer respects a profession. You've only to see how the country people stream into our sprawling towns . . .

LADY: Yes, Monsieur, I see.

GENTLEMAN: . . . When there's no respect for a profession, there's none for a child, and the child, if you don't find I express myself too strongly, is the father of the man.

LADY: Quite true.

GENTLEMAN: Perhaps too the child has forgotten how to win respect!

LADY: Perhaps.

GENTLEMAN: And yet we ought to respect a child, for if there weren't any children, the human race would very soon die out.

LADY: That's what I was thinking! . . .

GENTLEMAN: Loss of respect for one thing leads to another and in the end you don't even respect your own word, when you give it.

LADY: It's terrible!

GENTLEMAN: It's all the more serious when you think that
the Word is divine, like the Word of God, we've no right
to take it lightly . . .

LADY: I agree with you perfectly. That's exactly why I
wanted to be sure my daughter had a sound education
and a respectable profession, so she can stand on her own
feet, earn an honourable living and learn to respect others
by starting with herself.

GENTLEMAN: You've been very wise. What has she been
doing?

LADY: She's gone a long way with her studies. I've always
longed for her to be a typist. So has she. She's just got her
diploma. She's going to join a firm that deals in fraudu-
lent transactions . . .

GENTLEMAN: She must be very proud and happy.

LADY: She's dancing for joy from morning to night. She's
worked so hard, poor little soul!

GENTLEMAN: Now she's won the reward for her labours.

LADY: It only remains for me now to find her a good
husband.

GENTLEMAN: She's a fine girl.

LADY: [*looking out into the wings*] Well now, there *is* my
daughter just coming. I'll introduce you to her.

 [*The* LADY's *daughter comes in. She is a man, about thirty
years old, robust and virile, with a bushy black moustache,
wearing a grey suit.*]

GENTLEMAID: Good morning, Mummy.

 [*A very strong masculine voice. The gentleman-daughter kisses
the* LADY.]

GENTLEMAN: She's the spitting image of you, Madame.

LADY: [*to* GENTLEMAID] Go and say good morning to the
gentleman.

GENTLEMAID: [*curtseying first*] Good morning, Monsieur!

GENTLEMAN: Good morning, my dear! [*To the* LADY:] She's really very well brought-up. How old is she?

LADY: Ninety-three!

GENTLEMAN: She's passed her majority then?

LADY: She owes us eighty years, so that makes her only thirteen.

GENTLEMAN: They'll pass, you know, as quickly as the others! [*To the* GENTLEMAID:] Well now, so you're a minor?

GENTLEMAID: [*in a very powerful voice*] Yes, but don't forget: Many a minor mates a major!

[*The* GENTLEMAN *and the* LADY *rise to their feet horrified. They all look at each other petrified, the* LADY *with clasped hands.*]

CURTAIN